The Love of Christ

Agnes Gonzha Bojaxhiu, now known as Mother Teresa of Calcutta, was born on 27 August 1910, of Albanian parents, at Skopje, Yugoslavia, and at the age of 15 was inspired by a missionary's letters to volunteer for the Bengal Mission. In 1928 she went to Loreto Abbey, Rathfarnham, Dublin and from there to India to begin her novitiate. From 1929 to 1948 she taught at St Mary's High School in Calcutta, for some years being Principal of the school, as well as being in charge of the Daughters of St Anne, the Indian religious Order attached to the Loreto Sisters.

In September 1946 Mother Teresa asked permission to live alone outside the cloister and to work in the Calcutta slums. Two years later she first put on the white sari with the blue border and cross on the shoulder which has become so well-known. After a further two years the new congregation of the Missionaries of Charity was approved and instituted in Calcutta in October 1950.

Now Mother Teresa's work has spread to many needy parts of the world, and has been recognized by various honours, including the Pope John XXIII Peace Prize in 1971 and the Nobel Peace Prize in 1979.

Available in Fount Paperbacks

By Mother Teresa

A GIFT FOR GOD

About Mother Teresa

MOTHER TERESA:
HER PEOPLE AND HER WORK
by Desmond Doig

SOMETHING BEAUTIFUL FOR GOD
by Malcolm Muggeridge

Mother Teresa
of Calcutta

The Love of Christ

SPIRITUAL COUNSELS

Edited by Georges Gorrée
and Jean Barbier

Collins
FOUNT PAPERBACKS

First published in the USA by Harper & Row, Publishers, Inc., in 1982. First published in Great Britain by Fount Paperbacks, London, in 1982.

Parts I and II were translated by John A. Otto from the original French edition, *Tu M'Apportes l'Amour* (Paris, Les Editions du Centurion, 1975). Parts III and IV are based on Mother Teresa's original English documents.

Made and printed in Great Britain by William Collins Sons & Co Ltd, Glasgow.

Contents

Introduction

Mother Teresa speaks little, publishes even less. Of
necessity, however, she carries on a large volume of
correspondence. In addition, she is asked for many
interviews and sometimes has to speak in public
(whenever her work is recognized by a prize of one
kind or another). In this varied activity, in which she
is generally spontaneous and uninhibited by the fear
of repetition, what she projects is the faith by which
she lives and love that impels her.

Appearing in this work are words of Mother Teresa.
Some of them have been gathered by attentive listen-
ers. Others are drawn from her letters, or from direc-
tives to her Co-Workers, or from her commentary on
the constitutions of the Missionary Sisters and Brothers of Charity. Our aim has been to reproduce her
simple and straightforward language, which concen-
trates on the truly essential and reveals the beauty of
a totally dedicated life as well as the almost unbeara-
ble realities of misery and suffering.

As an aid to the reader, some division into parts had
to be made. The division, in the nature of the case, is
more or less arbitrary. Mother Teresa's life, however,

is not divided or compartmentalized. It is an indivisible whole, its source and strength the twofold commandment of love of God and love of neighbor.

Acknowledgments

Some of the material in Parts I and II is drawn from Malcolm Muggeridge's *Something Beautiful for God* (New York, Harper & Row, 1971) and the authors' earlier work on Mother Teresa, *Amour sans frontière*.

The text of Parts III and IV is from unpublished material that was supplied by the Missionaries of Charity.

In addition, we have drawn upon interviews given by Mother Teresa and articles by various journalists such as Ralph Rolls and Sandro Bordignon.

PART I

God

MY LIFE, BUT NEVER MY FAITH

"Lord, give me this vision of faith, and my work will never become monotonous."

> *So prays Mother Teresa, in prayer both strong and confident. Ralph Rolls asked her what she would do if a country where she worked demanded that she give up her faith. She replied:**

No one can take my faith from me. If, in order to spread the love of Christ among the poor and neglected, there were no alternative but to remain in that country, I would remain—but I would not renounce my faith. I am prepared to *give up my life but never my faith.*

> *Voluntarily choosing this hazardous and humanly wretched life is the measure of her faith. What else explains it? Certainly not the results,*

---

* Material in italics is commentary by the authors. The rest of the text is Mother Teresa's own words.

> *which, as the world counts, would have to be judged small.*

We realize that what we are accomplishing is a drop in the ocean. But if this drop were not in the ocean, it would be missed. If we did not have our schools in the quarters of the poor—they are small, primary schools, where we teach the children to like school and how to keep themselves clean—if we did not have these small schools, the thousands of children who benefit from them would be left in the streets.

It is the same with our Home for the Dying. If we did not have this home, those whom we bring in would die in the streets. I believe it is worth the trouble to have this home, if only for the comparatively few we can handle, so that they may die with some dignity and in the peace of God.

> *Another secret of Mother Teresa's life is her power of perseverance. According to the French priest-orator Lacordaire, to persevere one must be as "loving as a mother and as hard as a diamond." Mother Teresa finds the explanation in her faith:*

Faith is a gift of God. Without it there would be no life. Our work, to bear fruit, to belong only to God, to be deserving, must be built on faith.

Christ said: "I was hungry, I was naked, I was sick, I was homeless, and you did that for me."* All our work is based on faith in these words.

---

* Matthew 25:35-40: "'For I was hungry and you gave me food, I was thirsty and you gave me drink, I was a stranger and you welcomed me, I was naked and you clothed me, I was sick and you visited me, I was in prison and you came to me.' Then the righteous will answer him, 'Lord, when did we see thee hungry and feed thee,

If faith is lacking, it is because there is too much selfishness, too much concern for personal gain. For faith to be true, it has to be generous and loving. Love and faith go together; they complete each other.

| *But she does not impose her faith.*

It is our prayer that Christ communicate His light and life to each of us and through us to the world of misery. We hope that the poor, whatever their beliefs, seeing us will be drawn to Christ and will want us to come to them, into their lives.

Mother Teresa's faith is something so absolute and so solid that she would rather see herself and her work destroyed than forget her faith or doubt it for a moment. The intensity of her faith is a phenomenon that is attracting the attention of the world and making history. Faith exudes from her whole being, faith that is truth.

Though reason retains its importance in the exercise of faith and following Christ does not mean its abandonment, the young, beset with problems, sometimes forgo the reasoning process. In the case of Mother Teresa, at least, they seem to follow her implicitly.

When she decided to join a march of seven kilometers through the streets of Milan for the purpose of arousing support for solidarity with the

or thirsty and give thee drink? And when did we see thee a stranger and welcome thee, or naked and clothe thee? And when did we see thee sick or in prison and visit thee?' And the King will answer them, 'Truly, I say to you as you did it to one of the least of these my brethren, you did it to me.' "

> *Third World, for her, according to the French*
> *journalist Bordignon, it was a symbolic gesture.*
> *The organizers had been preoccupied with the de-*
> *tails of the march, but the news that she would*
> *participate transformed it into a procession of*
> *faith. Everyone was struck by the expression on*
> *her face, the ascetical features which, like her*
> *words, spoke the force of truth. Afterwards she*
> *was received by Cardinal Giovanni Colombo,*
> *archbishop of Milan, to whom she said:*

Before God we are all poor.

> *Why this march? Why would thousands of young*
> *people assemble at the cathedral square to begin*
> *with Mother Teresa this seven-kilometer march*
> *without fanfare, without banners? Why would the*
> *young march for something they did not clearly*
> *understand, or if they did, still hesitated to admit*
> *it for fear of being challenged?*

The young are the builders of tomorrow. Youth today is in search of selflessness, and when it finds it, is prepared to embrace it.

In Harlem a young woman of a wealthy family came to us in a taxicab and told me: "I have given everything to the poor and have come to follow Christ."

Sometimes Jesus receives unusual attention. One evening in London I had a telephone call from the police: "Mother Teresa, there is a women in the streets very drunk, who is calling for you." We went to find her and on the way back she said to me: "Mother Teresa, Christ changed water into wine so that we would have some to drink." And she was very, very drunk!

> *Ralph Rolls put this question to Mother Teresa: "Is it important for you to be a Catholic?"*

Yes. For me and for every individual, according to the grace God has given to each.

> *It matters little, then, to what part of the Christian church we belong?*

No, it is important for the individual. If the individual thinks and believes that his or her way is the only way to God, if they do not know any other way, do not doubt and so do not feel the need to look elsewhere, then that is their way of salvation, the way that God comes into their life. But from the moment that a soul receives the grace to know God it must begin to seek. And if it does not seek, it moves away from the right road. But God gives to all souls that He creates a chance to meet Him and to accept Him or reject Him.

> *Is unity among Christians important?*

Yes, because Christians represent a light for others. If we are Christians, we must resemble Christ. I believe this very deeply. Gandhi once said if Christians had lived their Christian life completely, there would be no Hindus left in India. People expect us to live our Christian life fully.

> *The followers of other religions, Moslems, Hindus, are they also blessed by God and does God work through them too?*

God has His own means and ways of working in the hearts of people, and we do not know how close they are to Him. But in their actions we always have a clue to their attitude toward Him, whether or not they are responsive to Him. Moslem, Hindu, or Christian, the way you live your life is the measure of your belonging to God. We cannot condemn or judge, or speak words that might hurt. Perhaps a person has never heard of Christianity; if so, we do not know in what manner God appears in this soul and in what way He has this soul serve His purpose. By what right, then, can we condemn anyone?

I LOOK UPON HIM, HE LOOKS UPON ME

It is not possible to engage in the apostolate without being a soul of prayer, without consciously forgetting oneself and submitting to God's will. We must be conscious of our oneness with Christ, as He was of His oneness with His Father. Our activity is truly apostolic only to the extent that we let Christ work in us and through us, with all His power, all His desire, and all His love.

> *A soul of prayer can make progress without recourse to words, by learning to listen, to be present to Christ, and to look toward Him.*

Often we do not receive what we prayed and hoped for because we did not fix our attention and our hearts on Christ, through whom our prayers come to God. Many times a deep and fervent gaze upon Christ is the best prayer. *I look upon Him, He looks upon me* is the most perfect prayer.

| *Her prayer speaks mercy, kindness, patience.*

"Lord, grant that I may always bear in mind the very great dignity of my vocation, and all its responsibilities. Never let me dishonor it by being cold, or unkind, or impatient."

Love prayer. Feel often the need to pray, and take the trouble to pray. It is by praying often that you will pray better. Prayer enlarges the heart until it is capable of containing the gift that God makes of Himself. Ask and seek: your heart will grow capable of receiving Him and holding on to Him.

| *The need to discover Christ in the sick forms part*
| *of her daily prayer.*

"Jesus, my suffering Lord, grant that today and every day I may see You in the person of Your sick ones, and that in caring for them I may serve You. Grant also that even in the guise of the fretful, the demanding, the unreasonable, I may still recognize You and say: My suffering Jesus, how sweet it is to serve You.

"Lord, give me this vision of faith, and my work will never become monotonous. I will find joy in indulging the moods and gratifying the desires of all the poor who suffer.

"O dear sick one, how much dearer still you are to me because you represent Christ. What a privilege I have to be able to tend to you.

"O God, since You are Jesus in his suffering, deign

also to be to me a patient Jesus, overlooking my faults, seeing only my intentions, which are to love You and to serve You in the person of each of Your children who suffers. Lord, increase my faith.

"Bless my efforts and my work, now and always."

| *"How do you pray?" Bordignon asked her.*

We begin our day by seeing Christ in the consecrated bread, and throughout the day we continue to see Him in the torn bodies of our poor. We pray, that is, through our work, performing it with Jesus, for Jesus, and upon Jesus.

The poor are our prayer. They carry God in them. Prayer means praying everything, praying the work.

| *What consolation do you find in your work?*

We meet the Lord who hungers and thirsts, in the poor . . . and the poor could be you or I or any person kind enough to show us his or her love and to come to our place.

IN SILENCE, HE HEARS US, HE SPEAKS TO US

It is very hard to pray if one does not know how. We must help ourselves to learn.

The most important thing is silence. Souls of prayer are souls of deep silence. We cannot place ourselves directly in God's presence without imposing upon ourselves interior and exterior silence. That is why we must accustom ourselves to stillness of the soul, of the eyes, of the tongue.

God is the friend of silence. We need to find God, but

we cannot find Him in noise, in excitement. See how nature, the trees, the flowers, the grass grow in deep silence. See how the stars, the moon, and the sun move in silence.

Is not our mission to bring God to the poor in the streets? Not a dead God but a living God, a God of love. The apostles said: "We will devote ourselves to prayer and to the ministry of the word."

The more we receive in our silent prayer, the more we can give in our active life. Silence gives us a new way of looking at everything. We need this silence in order to touch souls. The essential thing is not what we say but what God says to us and what He says through us.

Jesus is always waiting for us in silence. *In this silence He listens to us; it is there that He speaks to our souls.* And there, we hear His voice. Interior silence is very difficult, but we must make the effort to pray. In this silence we find a new energy and a real unity. God's energy becomes ours, allowing us to perform things well. There is unity of our thoughts with His thoughts, unity of our prayers with His prayers, unity of our actions with His actions, of our life with His life.

Our words are useless unless they come from the bottom of the heart. Words that do not give the light of Christ only make the darkness worse.

Make every effort to walk in the presence of God, to see God in everyone you meet, and to live your morning meditation throughout the day. In the streets in particular, radiate the joy of belonging to God, of living with Him and being His. For this reason, in the streets, in the shelters, in your work, you should always be praying with all your heart and all your soul. Maintain the silence that Jesus maintained for thirty years at Nazareth, and that He still maintains in the tabernacle, interceding for us. Pray like the Virgin Mary, who kept all things in her heart through prayer and meditation, and still does, as mediatrix of all graces.

Christ's teaching is so simple that even a little child can learn it. The apostles said: "Teach us to pray." Jesus answered: "When you pray, say, Our Father . . ."

ALONE, WE CAN DO NOTHING

Mother Teresa chooses to serve. But service she understands as an instrument that is more effective the more humble it is.

That is why we should be able to summon our courage and say in all sincerity: "I can do all things in Him, because it is He who strengthens me."

This assertion of St. Paul should give you great confidence in the realization of your work, or rather God's work, in its efficacy and perfection in Jesus and for Jesus. Be also convinced that alone, of yourself, you can do nothing, and have nothing except sin, weakness and misery; that all the natural gifts and gifts of grace we have were given to us by God.

We can see the humility of Jesus in the crib, in the Exile in Egypt and His hidden life, in the inability to make Himself understood by people, in the abandonment by the apostles, in the hatred of His enemies

among the Jews, in all the bitter sufferings of the
Passion, and now in His acts of constant humility in
the tabernacle, where he reduces Himself to such a
small piece of bread that the priest can hold Him
between two fingers.

> *To Malcolm Muggeridge she made the request
> that his study about her work not be in the nature
> of a biography of herself:*

The life of Christ was not written during his lifetime, yet He did the greatest work on earth—He redeemed the world and taught mankind to love His
Father. The work is His work and to remain so, all of
us are but his instruments, who do our little bit and
pass by.*

Let there be no pride or vanity in the work. The
work is God's work, the poor are God's poor. Let us put
ourselves completely under the power and influence
of Jesus, so that He may think with our minds, work
with our hands, for we can do all things if His strength
is with us.

Our mission is to convey the love of God, who is not
a dead God but a living God.

> *Not a God of facile or premature solutions that
> seem reasonable but sometimes wound the sensi-
> tivity of people in distress. Not a dead God, served
> merely from a sense of duty, a burden on our con-
> science that we attempt to load onto the shoulders
> of others. But a living God, a God of mercy, of*

---

* Malcolm Muggeridge, *Something Beautiful for God* (New York:
Harper & Row, 1971), p. 15.

compassion, who in Jesus Christ took the form of man and became a member of the poor.

Mother Teresa teaches us that the desire to serve the poor requires that we acknowledge the misery in ourselves, our own insufficiency and radical poverty.

We must accept our vulnerability and limitations in regard to others. This is essential in gaining their confidence. We cannot expect to help others from the "outside."

Learn to be quiet so that the other can speak. Forget about rules that relegate the oppressed to the margins of society, leaving them in their isolation. Hope with the captives of unjust social conditions, who have nothing but their untold wants. Hope with "prisoners," those overwhelmed by physical, moral, or spiritual misery.

Mother Teresa permits herself to be "touched" by the untouchables, those whom we too quickly consign to the ranks of the irrecoverable, the hopeless. She permits herself to be "disarmed" by the exigent cry of people. Often it is the "marginalization," the rejection, the lack of understanding that causes people to withdraw into themselves.

It is not easy to be poor with the poor, to surrender power and the confidence in our "solutions," our "normality."

It is not easy to visit a person in his or her isolation, to break down the barriers that separate the world of the "haves" from the world of the "have-nots."

It takes a great deal of humility to acknowledge

> *one's limitations, one's helplessness or inade-*
> *quacy.*
>
> *One of Mother Teresa's favorite thoughts is:*

With Jesus, everything is possible because God is
love.

> *Despite the publicity and attention that surround*
> *her—which she does not want and tries to discour-*
> *age**—*Mother Teresa moves about in her unas-*
> *suming manner, slight and almost unnoticed*
> *amid the others.*
>
> *When one finds her, in an old building on the*
> *grounds of the Kali Temple, it is difficult to pick*
> *her out from the other Sisters. Nothing suggests*
> *that she is the founder of a congregation of reli-*
> *gious with foundations all over the world.*
>
> *She finds it painful to get ready for an inter-*
> *view. She confesses:*

For me, it is more difficult than bathing a leper, if
it comes to that.

> *Before a television interview she can be seen seated*
> *in a dim corner behind the curtain, fingering her*
> *large beads as she waits to speak to thousands, or*
> *millions.*

---

*Mother Teresa was recently quoted to the effect that the publicity
that has fallen on her since receiving the Nobel Prize was interfer-
ing with her work of service to the poor and therefore she would not
"participate in any more receptions" (United News of India, 2 April
1980). Nevertheless, her work continues to be recognized. In April
1980 she received the Bharat Ratna (Jewel of India), India's highest
civilian award, for her "exceptional service of charity" to the poor
of India's cities.—Translator's note.

She does not put her thoughts on paper or make notes. She does not have the gift for that kind of preparation; she relies for guidance on her rosary.

GIVE ME TO DRINK

Jesus thirsts for love. This same God who says that He does not need to tell us if He is hungry did not hesitate to ask for a drink of water from the Samaritan woman. But in saying, "Give me to drink," it was the love of His creature that the Creator asked for.

"What you do to the least of my brethren, you do to me." Mother Teresa develops this thought:

When I was hungry, you gave me to eat.
When I was thirsty, you gave me to drink.

Whatsoever you do to the least of my brethren, that you do unto me.
Now enter the house of my Father.

When I was homeless, you opened your doors.
When I was naked, you gave me your coat.

When I was weary, you helped me find rest.
When I was anxious, you calmed all my fears.

When I was little, you taught me to read.
When I was lonely, you gave me your love.

When in a prison, you came to my cell.
When on a sick bed, you cared for my needs.

In a strange country, you made me at home.
Seeking employment, you found me a job.

Hurt in a battle, you bound up my wounds.
Searching for kindness, you held out your hand.

When I was Negro, or Chinese, or white, and
Mocked and insulted, you carried my cross.

When I was aged, you bothered to smile.
When I was restless, you listened and cared.

You saw me covered with spittle and blood,
You knew my features, though grimy with sweat.

When I was laughed at, you stood by my side.
When I was happy, you shared in my joy.*

We must live this life, this hard life, to be able to
continue to work among the people. The work is our
only way of expressing our love for God. Our love must
pour on someone. The people are the means of expressing our love of God.

God gives what is needed. He gives to the flowers
and the birds, and to everything that He has created
in the universe. And the little children are His life.
There can never be enough of them.

If the work is seen only through our own eyes and
our own means, obviously we are not up to the task.
But in Christ we can do all things. That is why this
work has become possible, because we are convinced
that He, Christ, works with us and through us, in the
poor and for the poor.

The work is only an expression of the love we have
for God. Loving others is an expression of our love for
God.**

_____

* Reprinted from Muggeridge, *Something Beautiful for God,* pp.
78–79.
** Letter from Mother Teresa to Co-Workers, December, 1971.

We must all be witnesses of Christ. Christ is the vine and we are the branches. Without us, there would be no fruit. This is something to bear in mind. God is the vinedresser to all of us. Christ made no distinction between priests and brothers, sisters and laywomen, no distinction as witness-bound. We must all be witnesses of Christ's compassion, Christ's love, to our families, to our neighbors, to the towns or cities where we reside, and to the world in which we live.

Only in heaven will we know how much we owe to the poor, because on account of them we were able to love God more.*

> *For the poor, Mother Teresa renounces and empties herself. Were it not for Jesus Christ, this renunciation would seem absurd, an abdication of reason. But the poor invest it with Jesus Christ. Love of Jesus is the light that shines in her life and lends her a kind of spiritual luminosity which radiates from her in spite of herself and trails her wherever she goes. It lights up her wrinkled face and is the reason why the world is intrigued, yes, fascinated.*
>
> *Jesus is the one she wants her Co-Workers to bring to the world but especially to the poor.*

A Co-Worker must be capable of bringing Jesus to people. For that, we must remain close to God. We should have a daily holy hour of prayer and meditation. Even where we are not many, we could have it

---

* Mother Teresa, at the first national congress of Co-Workers held in Salt Lake City, Utah.

in our parish church, or wherever we are. If we truly love the poor, our first contact must be with Jesus, in the blessed sacrament. Then it will be easy to bring our love for Jesus to the poor.

> *"I am the bread of life; he who comes to me shall not hunger, and he who believes in me shall never thirst" (John 6:35).*
>
> *Mother Teresa strives to be one "body" with Jesus; her "food" is to praise His Name. To be one "body" with Jesus means to let oneself be touched and healed by His mercy, to have eyes to see,*
> *ears to hear,*
> *tongue to speak,*
> *to attack moral and physical corruption, to relieve spiritual and bodily paralysis.*
>
> *The "Body" of Christ is the prism through which she sees the body of the neighbor.*

Because we cannot see Christ, we cannot express our love to Him in person. But our neighbor we can see, and we can do for him or her what we would love to do for Jesus if He were visible.

Let us be open to God so that He can use us. Let us put love into our actions, beginning in the family, in the neighborhood, in the street. It is difficult, but there is where the work begins. We are co-workers of Christ, a fruitbearing branch of the vine.*

> *The street! With its surprises, its dens, hovels, and teeming misery! This where poverty roots. No*

---

* Mother Teresa, on receiving the Templeton Prize in London.

> *need for explanations, for big words. My brother or
> sister is there, waiting.*
>
> *The thoughts of the heart, does one write them
> down? That would be to rationalize them, to make
> them serve where they cannot serve. Love does not
> wait for explanations. It goes to work, a light, a
> force that finds new ways to meet the hopelessness
> of the old.*

We can work, but we cannot do it without God's
help. This we receive in our daily mass, when He gives
us strength through His bread.

> *She insists, to the chagrin of the world, that in
> dealing with the poor the tables are turned: it is
> not the poor who are indebted to us but we who are
> indebted to them.*
>
> *Mother Teresa explains what she considers to be
> the essential difference between the Christian and
> non-Christian conceptions of love.*

Non-Christians and Christians both do social work,
but non-Christians do it for something while we do it
for someone. This accounts for the respect, the love
and devotion, because we do it for God. That is why we
try to do it as beautifully as possible. We are in continual contact with Christ in His work, just as we are in
contact with Him at mass and in the blessed sacrament. There, Jesus has the appearance of bread. But
in the world of misery, in the torn bodies, in the children, it is the same Christ that we see, that we touch.

> *Accordingly, for Mother Teresa the two command-
> ments, love of God and love of neighbor, are*

> *fulfilled together; they are in fact inseparable. Her*
> *life is a monument to these two loves which are*
> *one. How, if we do not love God, can we love our*
> *neighbor; and how, if we do not love our neighbor,*
> *can we love God?*
>
> *She preaches Christ every moment of the day, by*
> *living in Him, through Him, and for Him.*
>
> *In 1956 Mother Teresa introduced the daily*
> *Holy Hour for her Co-Workers.*

To make a retreat, let Jesus work in you. Let there be exposition, scripture, silence.

Jesus asked his disciples to be with Him in His prayer. Finding them asleep, He said: "You can sleep now and take your rest. All is finished, the hour is come."

It is by an intuition of the heart that we are drawn to the Eucharist to come into His presence. The tabernacle is the guarantee that he has "pitched his tent" among us, perpetually.

The Eucharist is the sacrament of prayer, the source and summit of the Christian life. His presence before us hastens His cumulative presence in us. His presence imparts the Spirit to us, and lights up the shadows of our heart in deep communion.

The Holy Hour before the Eucharist should lead us to a "holy hour" with the poor, with those who will never be a human success and whose only consolation is Jesus. Our Eucharist is incomplete if it does not make us love and serve the poor. In receiving the communion of the poor, we discover our own poverty.

Every day we partake of the blessed sacrament, and

we have noticed a change come over our life. We have
experienced a deeper love for Christ in the distressful
appearance of the poor. We have come to a better
understanding of ourselves and a better understanding of the poor—a clear sign of God's blessing.

Since we began this devotion, we have not dimin-
ished our work. We spend as much time at it as before,
but now with greater understanding. People accept us
more, now, because they hunger for God. Their need
is not for us but for Jesus.

> *But how can one bring them Jesus unless oneself*
> *is intent on holiness?*

I WILL

Holiness consists in doing God's will joyfully. Faithfulness makes saints. The spiritual life is a union with
Jesus: the divine and the human giving themselves to
each other. The only thing Jesus asks of us is to give
ourselves to Him, in total poverty, and total self-for-
getfulness.

The first step toward holiness is the will to become
holy. Through a firm and upright will we love God, we
choose God, we hasten to God, we reach Him, we have
Him.

Often, under the pretext of humility, of trust, of
abandonment, we can forget to use the strength of our
will. Everything depends on these words: "I will" or "I
will not." And into the expression "I will" I must put
all my energy.

One cannot expect to become a saint without paying

the price, and the price is much renunciation, much temptation, much struggle and persecution, and all sorts of sacrifices. One cannot love God except at the cost of oneself.

If you learn the art of self-restraint and thoughtfulness, you will become more and more like Christ. His heart is all recompense, and He always thought of others. Jesus went about only doing good. At Cana, our Blessed Mother thought only of the needs of others and made them known to Jesus. The thoughtfulness of Jesus, Mary, and Joseph was so great that they made Nazareth a privileged abode of the Most High. If we had this same solicitude for one another, our communities would truly become a privileged abode of the Most High.

> *Mother Teresa is so closely united with God that God reveals Himself through her person. She is at once salt of the earth and light of the world. People who come to her are drawn to her in the same way that the crowds of Jerusalem were drawn to Christ.*
>
> *There is a brightness, a luminosity to Mother Teresa's love which overflows her Home for the Dying and transforms repellent and irritable creatures into human beings responding to love.*
>
> *A sort of "materialization" of this luminosity is reported by Malcolm Muggeridge, who was in charge of making a film about the Home for the Dying. The light inside was so dim that the cameraman said it was impossible to get a picture. It was decided to go ahead anyway. To the surprise*

> *of the technicians, the processed film showed the inside of the home and the dying bathed in beautiful soft light and was some of the best footage taken! What was the explanation for this "unnatural" occurrence?*
>
> *"I myself am absolutely convinced," says Malcolm Muggeridge, "that the technically unaccountable light is, in fact, the Kindly Light Newman refers to in his well-known hymn. . . . Mother Teresa's Home for the Dying is overflowing with love, as one senses immediately on entering it. This love is luminous, like the haloes artists have seen and made visible round the heads of the saints. I find it not at all surprising that the luminosity should register on a photographic film."**

Her light restores joy. Joy is a power, and the poor followed Jesus because power dwelled in Him, "went forth" from Him, flowed from His eyes, His hands, His body, totally given, present, to God, to people.

> *Malcolm Muggeridge relates that after his television interview with Mother Teresa the response of the British public was astounding. He himself received numerous letters, all of them as much as saying: "This woman spoke to me as no one ever has, and I feel I must help her."***

---

* Muggeridge, *Something Beautiful for God*, pp. 41–44.
** Ibid., p. 31.

PART II

The Other

LOVING THE OTHER

> *Mother Teresa's love is so great that she sees the neighbor as more beautiful than the reality suggests. She believes in love and produces love where there was none.*

The poor are God's gift; they are our love. Christ will not ask how much we did but how much love we put into what we did. There are many people who are spiritually poor. The spiritual poverty found in Europe, in America, is a heavy burden to bear. In these countries it is very difficult to convey a sense of God's love.

Our spiritual life is a life of dependence on God; its fruit is our work for the poor. We try to "pray" the work, doing it for Jesus, in Jesus and to Jesus.

The poor are "hope." By their courage they truly represent the hope of the world. They have taught us a different way of loving God by making us do our utmost to help them.

> *The role of the mother in the betterment of the individual is all-important. One of them complained to Mother Teresa that her children do not listen to her and asked what she should do. Mother Teresa replied:*

Mothers are the heart of the home; they build family life by wanting, loving, and taking care of their children. One time in London I came upon a young boy who was on drugs. I said to him: "You are very young and should not be out in the street at this hour of the night." He replied: "My mother does not want me because I have long hair, and that is why I am here."

An hour later I returned to the same place and was told that the boy had taken four different drugs. He had been hurried to the hospital and very likely was already dead.

Recently, in L—, a young woman of twenty-one years, who had been scolded in the morning, attempted suicide later in the day by swallowing kerosene. Taken to the hospital, she said to the priest: "My mother chased me out of the house and I did not know where to go; so I thought the best thing would be to kill myself."

Much suffering of young people is attributable to the family, and particularly to mothers. Mothers make the home a center of love. Their role is sometimes hard, but there is the example of the Blessed Virgin, who teaches us to be good with our children. We Missionaries of Charity also have to be mothers and make our communities happy homes.

> *"Truly, I say to you, as you did it to one of the least of these my brethren, you did it to me" (Matthew 25:40).*
>   Mother Teresa's desire is to:

Help people recognize God in the person of the poor.*

> *Though the possibility of knowing God rests on a certain resemblance between man and the God who took a human form, there is nothing in common between the infinite nature of God and the finite nature of man.*

Let each Sister and Brother grow in resemblance to Christ, so that in the world of today He may still live His life of compassion and human kindness. Your love of Christ is so admirable! Keep the light of Christ always shining bright in your hearts. He is the Love to love.**

Love is a fruit always in season, and no limit is set. Everyone can reach this love.

Are we convinced of Christ's love for us and of our love for Him? This conviction is like the sun's rays, which cause the sap of life to flow and make the flowers of holiness blossom. This conviction is the rock on which holiness is built by serving Christ's poor and lavishing on them what we would love to do for Him in person.

If we follow this way, our faith will grow, our convic-

---

* Cf. Constitution of the International Association of Co-Workers of Mother Teresa.
** Letter, January 1973.

tion will grow, and the striving for holiness will become our daily task.

God loves those to whom He can give the most, those who expect the most from Him, who are most open to Him, those who have most need of Him and count on Him for everything.

Our works of charity are only the fruit of God's love in us. That is why those who are most united with Him love their neighbor most.

Love of Christ should be a living bond between all of us. Then the world will know that we are true missionaries of charity.

Perhaps only a smile, a little visit, or simply the fact of building a fire for someone, writing a letter for a blind person, bringing a few coals, finding a pair of shoes, reading for someone, this is only a little bit, yes, a very tiny bit, but it will be our love of God in action.

In spite of the fact that this year we might have less to show, much less in donations, if we spread and radiate love of Christ more, if we give Christ who hungers not only for bread but also our love, our presence, our contact, then 1971 could be the year of the real explosion of the love that God brings to the world.

Without God, we are human beings who have nothing to offer except sorrow and suffering.

EVERY PERSON IS UNIQUE

In serving the needs of the poor the Co-Workers should give special attention to those who are unwanted and deprived of love. For the worst disease in the world is not leprosy or tuberculosis but the feeling of being unwanted, unloved, and abandoned by everyone.

The greatest sin is the lack of love and charity, the terrible indifference to those on the fringe of the social system, who are exposed to exploitation, corruption, want, and disease. Since each member of our Society is to become a co-worker of Christ in this world of misery, each one must understand what God and the Society expect.

Let the poor, seeing the Co-Worker, be drawn to Christ and invite Him into their homes and their lives.

Let the sick and suffering find in the Co-Worker a veritable angel of comfort and consolation. And in the streets, let the little children cling to her because she reminds them of Christ who is the friend of little children.

> *When Mother Teresa, with only a few rupees in her pocket, went into the most wretched quarters of Calcutta to begin her work of love, we can imagine not only the courage it took but the tact and discretion. The people who confronted her were "hurt" individuals, unwanted, unloved, spurned or ignored by society, whose needs had to be prudently unearthed, sometimes with difficulty, because a hurt individual does not easily open up to a stranger but more likely masks his or her need behind suspicion, distrust, and outright antagonism. For this sort of work, Mother Teresa had to guard against having all the answers or quick and easy solutions.*

> *To help, without hurt to human dignity, means*
> *not only to move through the poor but to remain*
> *among them, live among them, and be a living*
> *expression of God's love.*
>
> *If Mother Teresa's efforts on behalf of the poor*
> *had come from a sense of duty, her words and her*
> *actions would not have conveyed the feeling of*
> *God's merciful love. The poor sensed the throb of*
> *her love in each of her actions. Those whom life*
> *has treated most cruelly are not deceived. They*
> *cannot be tricked or taken in by the semblance of*
> *love, by the person who shrinks from the risks of*
> *love.*
>
> *Mother Teresa was the first person who made*
> *them feel that someone really loved them and took*
> *an interest in them.*

If sometimes our poor people have had to die, it is
not because God did not take care of them but because
you and I have done nothing, have not been an instrument of love in God's hands; it is because we have
failed to recognize Him, Christ, when He came again
in the guise of distress, of a man or woman forsaken,
of a child abandoned.

Some time ago a little child came to our house about
midnight. I went down and there stood this little one
in tears. Upon questioning she said: "I went to my
mother and she did not want me; I went to my father
and he did not want me. You, do you want me?"

Here, in Melbourne, there are forlorn people who
are not loved; yet these people are God's . . . and they
are ours. In India, in Europe, wherever our Sisters

meet Christ in this pitiable disguise, it is the same hunger. Perhaps here in Australia, and in America, it is not hunger for a piece of bread or a bit of cloth to cover themselves; but there is this great loneliness, this terrible need: the feeling of being unloved, of having no one to turn to.

In Calcutta we have given refuge to more than 27,-000 persons from the street.* They come to us and we receive them, or we go out and bring them in and make them feel at home. They die so admirably . . . so admirably in the peace of God. Up to now, our Sisters and I myself have never yet seen or met a man or woman who refused to ask "pardon of God," who refused to say "I love you, my God."

We have thousands of lepers. They are so brave, so admirable, disfigured as they are. Last Christmas I went to see them and said to them that they have God's care, that God loves them specially, that they are very dear to Him and their malady is not sin.

An old man who was completely disfigured came up to me and said: "Repeat that again; it does me good. I had always heard that no one loves us. It is wonderful to know that God loves us. Say it again."

We have a Home of Mercy. We have people who have no one, who roam the streets, for whom perhaps prison and the street are the only refuge.

One of them had been seriously wounded by one of his friends. Somebody asked him: "Who did that to you?" The man began to tell all sorts of lies but would not say who did it. Later, when there was no one

---

* In 1975, more than 30,000.

around, I asked him: "Why didn't you say who
wounded you?" The man looked at me and said: "His
suffering would not help mine."

TRUE LOVE

*On receiving the Nehru Prize, Mother Teresa un-
derscored the importance of "true love."*

Love, to be true, must first be for our neighbor. This
love will bring us to God. What our Sisters, our Brothers and our Co-Workers across the world try to do is
to show this love of God by deeds. To help the poor we
must get to know them. Some persons who came to
help us with the problems of the refugees of Bangladesh said that they had received more than they
gave to those whom they had served.

This is exactly what each of us experiences when
we are in contact with the poorest of the poor. This
contact is what our people need. They need our
hands to serve them and our hearts to love them.
Think of the loneliness of old people, without means,
without love, with absolutely no one to care about
them. There are many places where we can see this
suffering, this hunger for love, which only you and I
can satisfy.

Think of forsaken children. One day I saw a little
child that would not eat; her mother had died. Then
I found a Sister who looked like her mother and I told
her just to play with the child, and the child's appetite
returned.

Responding to Prince Philip, who had presented her with the Templeton Prize, Mother Teresa said:

Dear Co-Workers, let us give thanks to God that Mr. Templeton has had the courage to dispense for God's glory the wealth he received so generously from God. Giving me this prize is giving it to all who are partners with me, across the world, in the work of love.

Here in England, how many isolated individuals there are, known only by their house number. So where do we start? Do we really know if there is someone, perhaps next door to us? Perhaps there is a blind person who would be happy if someone read the paper to him or her. Perhaps there is a wealthy individual who has no one to visit him. He has much other wealth, but he is lost in it. There is no human contact, and he needs your contact. Some time ago a very wealthy man came to us and said: "See this? I want to give it to you so that someone will come and visit us. I am half blind, and my wife is depressed; our children have left us to go abroad and we are dying of loneliness."

And in Melbourne I paid a visit to an old man no one knew existed. I saw that his room was in horrible condition and I wanted to clean it up, but he stopped me: "I'm all right." I kept quiet, and finally he let me go ahead. In his room was a beautiful lamp, covered with dust. I asked: "Why don't you light the lamp?" He replied: "What for? Nobody comes to see me, and I don't need a lamp." Then I said to him: "Will you light the lamp if the Sisters come to see you?" "Yes," he said, "if I hear a human voice, I will light it." The other day he sent me word: "Tell my friend that the lamp she lit in my life burns constantly."

These are the people we must learn to know. Knowing them will bring us to love them and to love helping them. We must not be satisfied with gifts of money. Money is not enough. Money can be got. But they need your hands to help them; they need your hearts to love them.

Very often I ask for gifts other than money. I can get these things if I want them, but I ask for them in order to get the presence of the donor, just to touch those to whom he or she gives, just to smile on them, just to give them some attention. That means so much to our people!

It is the same Jesus who met Saul on his way to Damascus to stir up trouble and kill and destroy Christians, and who said: "Saul, Saul, why do you persecute me?" And to whom Saul replied: "Who are you, Lord?" "I am Jesus whom you persecute."

And today, it is the same Christ, the same Jesus, in our poor who are unwanted. They are of no use to society, and nobody has time for them. It is you and I, if our love is true, who must seek them out.

The first time I was in London I went out at night. It was a very cold night and we met people in the street. There was a respectable old man shivering from the cold. With him was another old man, a black, who had opened his coat to wrap it around the other man against the cold. "Take me away, anywhere," the first man said to the other; "I would like to sleep between two sheets." He was a distinguished looking man who must have known better days, but there he was. And we looked around, and we saw many others.

And if there had been only one, it is Jesus. And, as Scripture says: "I looked for someone to care for me and I could find none." How terrible it would be if Jesus had to say that to us today.

Without the chance to receive the message of religious thought, even the most honest and most intelligent mind is really nothing more than a bee caught in a bottle.

I want people to get involved in the actual work we do, for their own sakes and for ours. I never ask them for money, nothing like that. I only ask them to bring their love, to bring their hands to help. Then, when they meet those in need, their first reaction is to do something for them. And when they come the second time, they already are committed. After a while, they feel that they belong to the poor; they understand their need for love, who they are, and what they themselves can do for them.

> *Love must be real. The reality of love is in the tongue that is not afraid to open up, in the offer to help that makes one vulnerable to the other, in the deed that treats the poor as equals. It says to the other, "you exist."*
>
> *Every person has the right to a minimum of goods for "security," but still more to justice, to growth, to free speech. Every person has the right to be "unique," to be an individual with human dignity.* *

* International Constitution, 6.

To humor the fancies of the poor is to begin with them from where they are, to take them by the hand so they may know they are thought of, counted on, "needed."

> *There the leper stood, straight up, in his arms a small basket of cabbage. In his arms, because on his hands not a single finger was left. He said to the Father of the lepers (Father Raoul Follereau): "I have lost my fingers and my hands, but I have kept my courage. I wanted to be someone, someone who works and sings, as you have said to us. So I learned to help myself with my hands—and without hands. A hundred times the tool fell to the ground. A hundred times I got down on my knees to pick it up. I have just brought in my first vegetables. I give them to you, because it is you who taught me that I was not an unwanted."*

We shall never know all the good that a simple smile can do.

We speak of our God, good, clement, and understanding; but are we the living proof of it? Those who suffer, can they see this goodness, this forgiving God, this real understanding in us?

Never let anyone come to you without coming away better and happier. Everyone should see goodness in your face, in your eyes, in your smile.

In the dispensaries, in the slums, wherever we are, we are the light of God's goodness.

Thoughtfulness, the kindly regard for others, is the beginning of holiness. If you learn the art of being thoughtful, you will be more and more like Christ; His heart was kind and gentle, and He always thought of others. Our vocation, to be beautiful, must be full of regard for others. Jesus did good wherever He went. Our Lady at Cana thought only of the needs of others and told Jesus about them.

I AM A MAN

The Co-Workers recognize the dignity, the individuality, and the infinite value of every human being.*

> *Sandro Bordignon, the French journalist, says of Mother Teresa: "I believe that no other philosopher or humanist has such a lively sense of the humanity and the value of every human being. The presence of the mayor, the cardinal, the leper, or anyone of the poor, it makes no difference; she meets and treats them with the same respect."*
>
> *Above all else, the poor one is a person. And if works of charity are collective, charity itself is individual.*
>
> *Ladies of fashion may meet in thick-carpeted homes, draw up their monthly schedule of philanthropies, make a financial report and see the slums from afar, like the tourist viewing the city below. This is necessary but not enough. From her Co-Workers Mother Teresa demands direct contact with the poor: visiting them in person, cleaning their homes, dressing their wounds. Charity is*

* Constitution, 6.

*directed toward someone, toward a person. When
the poor "hit bottom," they can lose the idea that
they are human beings.*

*Father Raoul Follereau tells of a leper who
tried to take advantage of the revulsion his condition can inspire. One evening, seeing some women
alone, he went up to them and said: "Give me
money or I will touch your faces and you will be
lepers." Terrified, the women complied. Father
Raoul heard about it and gave him a tongue lash-
ing for his efforts. But the culprit had nothing to
say. Worse, there was no sign of remorse. Finally
the priest, beside himself, yelled out: "Yes or no,
are you a man?" The leper straightened up and,
his eyes glistening, said: "You are right. I did
wrong. I am a man." And because he had been
treated as a "man," he added: "Thanks."*

*To love one's neighbor the way Mother Teresa
does it is necessary to dismiss all thought of ine-
quality. She sees the face of Christ in the leper as
well as in the radiant beauty of a little child. And
she believes in the person-to-person relationship.*

What is important to us is the individual. To get to
love a person, there must be close contact. If we wait
for the numbers, we will be lost in the numbers, and
we will never be able to show that person the necessary love and respect. Every person is for me the only
person in the world at that moment.

I believe that people today think the poor are not
humans like them. They look down on them. But if

they had a deep respect for the poor, I am sure it would be easy for them to come closer to them, and to see that they have as much right to the things of life and to love as anybody has. In these times of development, everybody is in a hurry and rushing about, and on the way there are people falling down, people who do not have the strength to run. It is these that we want to help and take care of.

I never take care of crowds, only of a person. If I stopped to look at the crowds, I would never begin. Love is a fruit always in season.

> *To make herself accepted, Mother Teresa identifies with the poor. She eats the same food, wears the same clothes.*
>
> *At the Congress of 1973, in Melbourne, Mother Teresa spoke of Christ identifying Himself with the sick, the naked, the homeless, the hungry.*

Hungry, not only for bread but also to exist for someone; naked, not only for lack of clothing but also lack of compassion, since very few people have compassion for the nameless multitude; homeless, not only having no home of wood or stone but no friendly soul of whom one can say "I have someone."

Our little children are in this category of the rejected and unloved. Today the problem that troubles so many people is not only the fear that the world is becoming overpopulated, but more and more we hear it argued that Providence cannot take care of all the babies that will be born.

For my part, if abortion is permitted in countries

that lack for nothing, these countries are the poorest of the poor. I would like to open in these countries many institutions for children. We have these small institutions all over India, and up to now we have never had to refuse a single child. And, most wonderfully, God has seen to it that each of these children that escaped death at the hands of their parents has found a home with new parents.

In Calcutta, we have tried to combat abortion by adoption, and we have been able to give many little ones who were destined to die a father and a mother. For us, in India, it is a wonderful thing, because by law these children are untouchables.

As for countries that have enacted laws permitting abortion as a so-called natural act, we must pray for them, because the sin is great. It is murder.

We were invited to Bangladesh to work with girls who had been abused by soldiers. Driven by despair and disgrace, some committed suicide. We opened a Home for Children for them, and had to overcome great difficulties, as it is against Moslem and Hindu law to take back into society girls like these who have been abused.

But when Mujibu said that these girls were national heroes, that they had tried to defend their purity and had fought for their country, their own parents came to get them. There were even young men who offered to marry them.

And then, some persons were asked to perform abortions on them. It was a terrible battle. I told them that these girls had been abused, forced, and had not wanted to sin, and that what some people wanted to do to them or help them do would be an act of murder. For the rest of their lives they would never forget that as mothers they had killed their children.

The government agreed with us, and it was announced that every child for which the mother had wanted an abortion should be brought to our home. Of the forty children we have received, more than thirty have been adopted by wonderful families. This is how we try to combat abortion.

Because our Sisters work in the slums, we have found more and more young mothers dying and children born deformed, and we could not find the reason. Looking deeper, we discovered that because of their ignorance these young women were being taken advantage of and abused. So we prayed to God to send us someone who could undertake the task of helping these women face this problem with a clean conscience, a healthy body in a happy family. We were blessed with the vocation we needed, a Sister from the Maurice Islands who had taken courses on natural family planning. We have begun the work of providing information, and today we have more than three thousand families putting it into practice, with a success rate of 95–96 percent.

When people saw what was happening in their families, they came to thank us. Some said: "Our family has remained together; our family is enjoying good health and we can have a baby when we want it."

*Ralph Rolls asked Mother Teresa what she had
been able to observe in England today on this subject. She replied:*

England seems to be hesitant about protecting unborn children and apparently tries to get rid of
them. They get rid of them by killing life; and to me,
that is an obvious sign either that the country is
very poor and does not have the means to take care
of lives that God has created, or that it has somehow
been misled.

*Rolls then asked her if she preferred that abortion
be illegal.*

I do not say legal or illegal, but I think that no
human hand should be raised to kill life, since life is
God's life in us, even in an unborn child. And I think
that the cry of these children who are killed before
coming into the world must be heard by God.

*Rolls asked how society could cope with so many
children, if they all came into the world.*

Jesus said that we are much more important in the
eyes of His Father than the grass, the birds, and the
flowers of the earth. And that if He takes care of these
things, how much more He would take care of His own
life in us. He cannot deceive us. Life is God's greatest
gift to human beings, and humans are created in the
image of God. Life belongs to God and we do not have
the right to destroy it.

*Our world tends toward the absurd, says Bordig-
non. We have created conditions of life un-*

*dreamed twenty years ago; we have increased
many times over the capacity to produce; we have
made unparalleled technological advances. In
view of this, it seems madness not to be able to feed
all the people in the world.*

*We are preoccupied with the demographic ex-
plosion and sometimes wonder what is to be
gained by saving the newborn infants that
Mother Teresa retrieves from the trash bins of
Calcutta. But then says Bordignon, I saw how
she thrilled when one of these tiny ones gave
signs of life. "It lives!" she exclaimed, and that
for Mother Teresa is joy.*

*She was also asked about the reasons for the
unexpected success of her natural family planning
efforts. She replied quite simply:*

People understood the usefulness of self-control.

BULLDOZER OF CHRIST

Deep faith in action is love, and love in action is service.

*Mother Teresa asks her Co-Workers to dedicate
themselves to wholehearted free "service" to the
poorest of the poor.**

I want the Co-Workers to put their hands and
hearts at the service of the people. If they do not
come in close contact with them, they cannot know
who the poor are. That is why, especially here in Cal-

* Constitution, 5.

cutta, we have a goodly number of non-Christians
and Christians working together in the Home for the
Dying and other places. Some groups prepare bandages and medicine for the lepers. For example, an
Australian came the other day to make a large donation. But after making the donation he said: "This is
something outside of myself; now I want to give
something of myself." Since then, he comes regularly to the Home for the Dying to shave the sick
and talk with them. He gives not only his money but
also his time. He could have spent both his money
and time on himself, but he wanted to spend himself
instead.

> *Mother Teresa's service is not aimless agitation,
> not helter-skelter activity lost in numbers. Rather,
> it is centered on Jesus, a single-minded service to
> Jesus in the guise of the poor.*
>
> *To serve, according to Mother Teresa, is to embrace and follow Christ the Servant. "I am with
> you as one who serves" (Luke 22:27).*
>
> *To serve is to be a servant of Christ present in
> the world, especially in his poor. The servant of
> Christ practices the compassion of Christ, which
> does not wait for gratitude. True compassion endures failure, conflict, thanklessness.*
>
> *To serve is to know and acknowledge the truth;
> to recognize the part that ignorance or innocence
> can play in those who fall; to give support rather
> than pass judgment; to be the voice of the voiceless; and never to yield to the temptation to be
> cross or unkind.*

To serve is to go to those who cannot render service for service, who show no gratitude, to those who are bitter, who suffer from lack of a kindly look, a smile. Mother Teresa stresses the power of a smile that communicates the joy of God.

Helping others ought to go further than the impersonal act of almsgiving. To give of our superfluity is not the same as giving of ourselves, or entering into the suffering of others.

Being rich or poor is not always a question of material possessions. Mother Teresa points out that distress, isolation, suffering can also be the lot of those who have material wealth. To serve is to take upon one's shoulders the burdens of others, to share their fears and anxieties.

Mother Teresa's service is a constant search for union with God. She serves God by serving others, children of God whose true worth she knows. Jesus bled for the poor. He wept.

Mother Teresa underlines the importance of being co-workers of Christ:

How much we ought to love our Society (the Missionaries of Charity) and show our gratitude by being what God and the Society expect of us: true co-workers of Christ. More than ever, we ought to do our work for Christ who was poor, and for the poor who are Christ's, with a humble and devoted heart.

In order to survive, love has to be nourished by sacrifices. The words of Jesus, "Love one another as I have loved you," must be not only a light to us but a flame that consumes the self in us.

Love should be as natural as living and breathing. The Little Flower said: "When I act and think charitably, I feel it is Jesus working in me; the deeper my union with him, the stronger my love for the residents of Carmel."

Mother Teresa's congregation has experienced an astonishing vitality. She accounts for this by saying:

We put our hands, our eyes, our hearts at Christ's disposal so that he may act through us.

She has been called a "bulldozer of Christ," because nothing stops her. Everything is urgent. From Calcutta Jean Vanier writes.

"I have just spent an hour with Mother Teresa. I was struck by her sense of urgency. She always seems to be returning from somewhere, New York, London, Rome, Gaza, the Yemen, Ethiopia, Amman. She spoke of Cambodia. Her acute sensitivity to the suffering in the world, which is almost an obsession, prods her to action. She was looking for a helicopter to bring food to the rural population of Ethiopia, and trying to find a way of helping Arabs and Israelis exchange their dead, as well as working out a plan to give assistance to the religious in Cambodia."

She had seen the prime minister of Israel and the ruler of Gaza. She was troubled by the hatred in the hearts of Arabs and Jews. She spoke of the suffering she had seen in London, and of her Home for the Dying in Calcutta, which has never been so full.

Could one set up a canteen at the railroad station in Saaldad for the starving?

> *Her creative talent is astonishing, always in search of solutions. Now she wants to see Madame Gandhi. Nothing is impossible. Her abandonment to God is total. Her wrinkled face shows great compassion—and fatigue; she has aged . . .*
>
> *But she is a "bulldozer of Christ." Nothing stops her. She is truly an instrument of God, and yet she is such a small woman . . .*
>
> *She does not like to speak of her community, of structures, only of the poor. One time she went to Rome for a meeting of Major Superiors and reported.*

But I said nothing. All the talk was about structures; I understood nothing. My mind was somewhere else.

> *She said this without a hint of criticism. In fact, I have never heard her make the least critical remark about anyone.*
>
> *No work is too much for Mother Teresa. Not content with washing feet, she repairs roofs damaged by the wind . . . and leads a march of seven kilometers through the streets of Milan to build solidarity with the Third World.*
>
> *She scarcely has time anymore to write to her Sisters:*

All my time is taken up by everybody; and with the Sisters it is the same. They work without interruption for the sick or the children and really do not have time to write. Tell the ailing Sisters not to be disappointed if they do not receive letters, because the work is all-consuming.*

LOVE ACCEPTS ALL AND GIVES ALL

Love and service are the key to giving.

> *"Freely have you received . . . freely give." Mother Teresa could say with one of our contemporaries: "I no longer belong to myself. Some evenings, after being worn out by others, I do not know who I am. I am someone else; I am God's."*

Love accepts all and gives all.

> *Mother Teresa's charity requires this total renunciation.*
> *In the constitution that governs her Co-Workers Mother Teresa declares:*

Co-Workers must recognize that all goods of this world are free gifts of God and that no one has the right to excess wealth when others are dying of hunger. Co-Workers seek to correct this grave injustice through voluntary poverty and the sacrifice of luxuries in their daily life.**

> *But Mother Teresa acknowledges that sometimes the wealthy make it a point to give.*

The wealthy, in their own way, do sometimes want to share in the misfortune of others. The pity is that

---

* Letter to Jacqueline de Decker.
** Constitution, 8.

they do not truly put themselves out. The new generation, especially the children, understand better. Children in England are making sacrifices to give a piece of bread to our children. Children of Denmark are making sacrifices to give them a glass of milk daily, and children of Germany are doing the same to give them daily vitamins. These are ways of learning to love. Children like these, when they grow up, will know what it means to give and will want to do so.

> *A beautiful display of "giving" is recounted by Sister Frederick. Students in a school in Canada went twenty-five hours without eating, in sympathy with those "who are starving." The pupils experienced what it means to go hungry and sent their impressions to Mother Teresa. Their only food was Christ, whom they received at a special Eucharist, celebrated at midnight.*
>
> *Another class arranged a "different experience," going without sleep for twenty-five hours. Like Christ, these young people bore in their flesh the cost of giving. Perhaps, through their sacrifice, somewhere in the world starving people were fed. It was their way of sharing in the suffering of others.*

We must suffer with Christ and that is why we want to share in the sufferings of the poor. Our congregation could die out in my lifetime, if the Sisters do not walk with the suffering Christ, and if the Sisters do not remain poor.

Our strict poverty is our safeguard. We do not want to begin by serving the poor and little by little end up serving the rich, like other religious orders in history. In order to understand and help those who lack everything, we must live like them. The difference is that our destitute ones are poor by force of circumstance, whereas we are by choice.

The Sisters do little things like help the children, visit the lonely, the sick, the poorest of the poor.

In one of the houses our Sisters visited, a woman living alone had been dead a long time before anyone knew it, and then they found out only because her corpse had begun to rot. Her neighbors didn't even know her name.

When someone says to me that the Sisters do not perform great tasks, that they do little things in their quiet manner, I reply that if they helped only one person, it would all be worth while.

Jesus died for one person, for one sinner.

> *Mother Teresa has no problem with culture, colonialism, or proselytism. When mass is celebrated with her poor in the pagan temple of Kali, no one takes offense. Rather, the emaciated worshippers, almost drained of life—so close are they to death—seem suffused with a sort of holiness, the holiness that is the sister of suffering and is not of this world.*

HAVING THE EXPERIENCE OF HAVING NOTHING

> *Mother Teresa exemplifies the call of Christ "not to lay up for yourselves treasures on earth, where*

*moth and rust consume and where thieves break
in and steal, but lay up for yourselves treasures in
heaven, where neither moth nor rust consume and
where thieves do not break in and steal" (Matthew
6:19).*

*In the Old Testament the prophet Isaiah directs
his maledictions against the wealthy of Jerusa-
lem: "Woe to those who join house to house, who
add field to field, until there is no more room, and
you are made to dwell alone in the midst of the
land . . . many houses shall be desolate, large and
beautiful houses, without inhabitant" (Isaiah 5:
8–9).*

*The spirit of poverty seen in the Missionaries of
Charity ought to remind the world of the prophet's
denunciations. A Mother Teresa is a standing rebuke to the mad pursuit of money.*

*For her activities on behalf of the poor she has
never accepted help from the state. She considers
her work a work of Providence.*

Even in the beginning, I never asked for money. I
wanted to serve the poor simply for love of God. I
wanted the poor to receive free what the rich get for
themselves with money.

*She regards wealth as an evil—worse than an evil,
a disaster—because it destroys generosity, closes
up the heart, suffocates. When, on occasion, she
appears in the homes of the rich, she has an un-
comfortable feeling of suffocation. When she was
invited to Washington by Senator Ted Kennedy,
the British writer St. John Stevas was present and*

*asked her how she felt in the midst of such opu-
lence. She replied that she was miserable, and
that she was there, in those beautiful drawing
rooms of Washington, only because someone had
to plead the cause of the poor.*

*But she does not condemn the rich. Instead of
passing judgment, she says:*

Who are we that we can judge the rich? Our task is
to bring the rich and the poor together, to be their
point of contact.

*Mother Teresa preaches revolution, but her idea
of revolution is not confrontation. Rather it is
the coming together, the mutually beneficial
meeting of the rich and the poor. Already she sees
results:*

Upper-caste families are adopting children we res-
cue from the streets, which is indeed revolutionary,
when one remembers the prejudice of the caste system. In this coming together the rich become better,
since they demonstrate love of God to the poor, and
the poor become better through the love they receive
from the rich.

*Mother Teresa dignifies the poor. A journalist
asked her who she thought was doing most for the
Gospel today: Pope John XXIII, Martin Luther
King, Gandhi . . .*

I believe that the most important person in the
world today is the poor person, since he or she has the
capacity to suffer and work hard.

> *To Mother Teresa, says Bordignon, the poor person is "the prophet of a new humanity." Perhaps we still worship the god of progress too much to appreciate the promise that her words hold for humanity.*
>
> *Tender-hearted and self-effacing, Mother Teresa carries an untiring charity in her heart, on her lips, in her look, and even in the elongated fingers so accustomed to dressing wounds. A burning love impels her to follow her Lord, to recognize Him in the peeping cry of an infant, in the wailing of a lost child, in the stumps of a leper, in the poor dying in the streets. A sensitive angel of mercy, she walked through Harlem with only a rosary in her hands for protection, in a quarter where no white dared to venture alone. Back in India, she moves among the dying,*

so that they may die seeing a kindly face and know there are people who love them and want to give them, at least in their final hours, a taste of human and divine love.

> *And also that they may have the comfort of seeing this woman bend over them and share the agony in their eyes, this woman who takes away fear and gives them a glance at the same little crucifix (the one she wears) that was kissed three times by a notorious criminal before his execution—as though in answer to the unknown prayers of St. Theresa of the Child Jesus. Of the dying she says:*

They lived like animals, but here they die like angels.

> *Mother Teresa's work is immense, but in her eyes so small as to be "a drop in the ocean."*
>
> *This drop, however, would be missed if it were not in the ocean. But she does not consider it a glittering drop. As she says:*

We do not strive for spectacular actions. What counts is the gift of yourself, the degree of love you put into each of your deeds.

> *This drop is the little tear that Mother Teresa, aglow with divine love, gathers from the eyelid of one who is dying.*

NO LOVE WITHOUT FORGIVING,
NO FORGIVING WITHOUT PEACE

> *This nun in a sari is so full of mercy that she attracts the poor because she is emptied of self in totally giving herself. She is not afraid to spend herself, to identify with her brother or sister in distress, or to launch into a career of mercy and forgiveness not counting the cost. She has met Christ in her work and teaches the lesson that we must forgive, since we have need to be forgiven.*

If we remember that we are sinners and have need of forgiveness, it is very easy to forgive others. If I did not understand that, it would be hard for me to say "I forgive you" to someone who comes to me.

Ralph Rolls asked if one had to be a Christian in order to forgive.

Not at all, not at all. Every human being comes from the hand of God and we all know how much God loves us. Whatever our belief, we must learn to forgive if we want truly to love. ·

Have you any evidence of this forgiveness?

Yes, I saw it in Belfast. Certain families I visited had lost members in the civil strife. These people forgave. They had neither hatred nor rancor toward those who had massacred their children.

> *The Missionary Brothers of Charity are doing wonderful work and having an influence on the lives of others. One young man had been a driver for a band of professional thieves. Seeing the work done by the Brothers in his neighborhood, he decided to change his way of life. He married a young woman who had been nursed back to health by the Brothers and now uses his leisure time to help them.*
>
> *It is a great thing to help build communities of love and goodness, which are signs of hope and strength. These signs may not be much in themselves, but they are filled with promise for peace and forgiveness in the world.*
>
> *In the encyclical* Pacem in Terris, *Pope John XXIII says: "Peace cannot reign among men unless it first reigns in each of them, that is, unless each observes in himself the order wanted by God."*

We must all work for peace. Before we can have this peace, we must learn from Jesus to be kind ánd humble of heart. Only humility can bring us to unity, and unity to peace. Therefore, let us help one another to draw so near to Jesus that we can learn with joy the lesson of humility.

Think of the oppressed countries. The greatest need in Bangladesh is for forgiveness. There is so much bitterness and hatred—you have no idea of what these poor people have suffered. If they could feel that someone cares about them, that they are loved, perhaps they would find it in their hearts to forgive. I believe that is the only thing that can bring peace.

We shall make this year a year of peace in a very special way. To this end we shall try to speak more to God and with God, and less to men and with men. Let us preach peace as Christ did. He went about doing good everywhere. He did not stop His works of charity because the Pharisees or others opposed Him and tried to destroy the work of His Father.

Cardinal Newman wrote: "Help me to spread your fragrance everywhere I go. Let me preach you without preaching, not by words but by my example; by the catching force, the sympathetic influence of what I do, the evident fullness of the love my heart bears to you."

SUFFERING AND JOYFULNESS

> *Not wanting Christ is the cause of suffering, today, in the world.*
>
> *Suffering can become a "gift," says Mother Teresa.*

Suffering in itself is nothing; but suffering that is sharing in the Passion of Christ is a wonderful gift, the most beautiful gift: a gift and proof of love, because in giving us his Son the Father showed that He loves the world. So, it proved that this was a gift, the greatest gift of love, because His suffering was the expiation for sin.

The suffering in Bangladesh is like an enormous Calvary, where the Body of Christ is crucified once more.

> *The barbarity of war scars the souls of people with a hatred that forgiveness, charity, and love alone can heal.*
>
> *In the appearance of those who have been "deformed" by suffering, Mother Teresa finds the outraged figure of Jesus: Jesus is present in those who are the despised and the outcasts of humanity. Jesus is transfixed in men and women of sorrow known only by their suffering, before whom we shield our eyes and flee.*
>
> *Classic outcasts from humanity, from whom we shrink and run away, lepers inevitably attracted the unfathomable love of Mother Teresa.*
>
> *Considerable progress has been made, however, in changing the attitude toward lepers. Leprosy is no longer seen as a disgrace but as a disease.*

At death we will not be judged by the amount of work we did but by the love we put into it. And this love must come from self-sacrifice and be felt until it hurts.

The heart of the work of the Missionaries of Charity

is committed to the four million lepers in the country. Leprosy is certainly a great evil, but not as great as being deprived of love or being unwanted or abandoned.

Lepers may be disfigured but they, like the poor, are wonderful people, with a great capacity for love.

> *Mother Teresa's love pours out on the victims of leprosy: young people and old, some of them unable to walk, reduced to crawling. She has discovered a feeling of community among them, a true comity of soul. Notwithstanding their offensive bodies, their ravaged faces, and rotting flesh, she finds in them a "hidden quality" that lends them human dignity. Working among them, she herself is so to speak transformed and becomes insensitive to the odor of the leprosarium. She forgets that she is among lepers. Appearances give way as the human person emerges. It is the person, not the leper that she knows and calls by name. She does not think of them as lepers but as individuals with their own names. Hers is a work of love, the fruit and sign of God's grace.*
>
> *Those who have seen Mother Teresa and her Sisters working in a leprosarium all testify that they are joyous and would not think of giving up this work. They love these lepers and follow them through their Calvary to the cemetery—the most pathetic funeral cortege one can imagine, behind an old rattling hearse with its plumed panels of glass.*
>
> *Pitiful scenes occur that tear at Mother Teresa's*

heart. A woman cared for at the leprosarium was told that her little girl also was leprous. The mother was beside herself, since she already had a boy in the leprosarium. The father came to see his family. The little girl limped toward him but stopped short of clasping his knees or throwing herself in his arms despite the overwhelming urge to do so. Remembering her condition, she just stood and stared at him. Her little body was diseased; her spirit, deprived of affection, died soon after. Occurrences like this make Mother Teresa say wherever she goes that the worst disease is not leprosy but the want of affection.

Other heart-rending scenes occur when lepers suffer the emotional trauma of leaving their homes to come to the leprosarium. One five-year-old in the leprosarium was there simply because two aunts who were leprous had caressed her when she was still a little child in the crib. The day she was taken away to the leprosarium brought a painful moment when she threw herself in the arms of her grandmother and said: "Will the Sisters love me like you? Will they hear my night prayers and tuck me into bed?"*

The sick can become close Co-Workers of a Sister or Brother by offering their suffering for that Sister or Brother.**

Each Sister should have a second self who prays and suffers for her; and each can draw from this support

---

*From information supplied by the Society of Mary.
**Constitution, 19.

a new strength and their lives will be like a burning
light that burns itself out for souls.

Suffering in itself is nothing, but suffering that
shares in the Passion of Christ is a wonderful gift
. . . and a sign of love.

How good God is to give you so much suffering and
so much love. All of this is joy to me and gives me
strength on account of you. It is your life of sacrifice
that gives me strength.

| *To the sick and dying she says:*

Your prayers and sufferings are like a chalice into
which we who are working can put, can pour, our love
for the souls that we meet. For this, you are just as
necessary as we; we and you, together, can do all
things in Him who strengthens us.

The vocation of suffering Sisters is a beautiful
thing. We are bearers of God's love. We carry in our
hearts and in our souls the love of God who thirsts
for souls. You can quench His thirst, you by your
priceless suffering, and we by our hard work. You
have known, you have tasted of, the chalice of His
agony.

| *To her Sisters she says:*

Without our suffering, our work would only be social work, very good and useful, but it would not be the
work of Jesus Christ. It would not be part of the Re-
demption. Jesus wanted to help us by sharing our life,
our loneliness, our agony, our death. It was necessary
that he become "one" with us in order to save us. He
permits us to do the same. The afflictions of the poor,

not only their material wretchedness but also their spiritual deprivation, must be redeemed and we must share their lives, because it is only by becoming "one" with them that we can save them, that is, bring God to them and bring them to God.

When suffering overtakes us, let us accept it with a smile. This is the greatest gift of God: having the courage to accept with a smile whatever He gives us and whatever He takes from us.

| *To an ailing woman she wrote:*

Very often I am near in thought to you, and I offer up your great sufferings when mine are small or trivial. When it is going very hard for you, then let your only refuge be in the Sacred Heart, and there my heart will find with you both strength and love. You want to suffer in pure love? Say rather in the love He chooses for you. How much I thank God for having given you to me. Give more and more, until you have no more to give.

My soul is heartened by the thought of having you to pray and suffer for me; I find it easier to smile. You do the suffering, we shall do the work. Together, we hold the same chalice in our hands.

> *I slept and I dreamed*
> *that life is all joy.*
> *I woke and I saw*
> *that life is all service.*
> *I served and I saw*
> *that service is joy!*
>   *(Nath Tagore)*

Mother Teresa said to an itinerant troupe called "Chant of Asia": We give joy to people by serving them; you, you give it by your performance. Your work and ours complete each other. What you do by singing and dancing, we do by scrubbing and cleaning. It is beautiful to be able to give joy to people. I am sure that thanks to you many people are comforted. And this talent you have received, only riches can deprive you of it. As long as you are willing to be empty of yourself and to be filled with God, you will keep this talent. The day that we begin to grow rich we lose something and begin to die.

Riches, material or spiritual, can suffocate you if they are not used in the right way. I praise God that you have followed your calling. Remain as "empty" as possible, so that God can fill you. Even God cannot put anything into what already is full. He does not impose Himself on us. It is you who are going to fill the world with the love God has bestowed on you. The work of moral rearmament goes on, prudently and with love. The more prudent the more effective it is. You bring it to people, and it is for them to absorb it. People are not so much interested in seeing us, but they hunger and thirst for what God wants to give them through us. We serve the same Lord. All over the globe, people hunger and thirst for God's love. In your way, you satisfy this hunger by spreading joy. In our way, we give joy by putting ourselves at the service of the sick, the dying, the rejected.

To Mother Teresa, conveying this joy is impera-
tive. A Sister asked if she could visit the poor.

| *Seeing the sad expression on her face, Mother Teresa said:*

Do not go. Go back to bed; we cannot meet the poor with a sad face.

| *Joy is "news" she wants to tell the world.*

In order to spread joy, it is necessary to have joy in one's family. Peace and war begin in the home. If we really want peace in the world, let us first love one another, in the family. We shall then have the joy of Christ, our strength. It is sometimes very hard to smile at one another. It is often hard for the husband to smile on his wife, or for the wife to smile on her husband.

Once I was asked if I was married; I said yes, and I added that it is sometimes hard for me to smile on Christ.

Attempts have been made to prove that God does not exist, but God is always proving that He does exist.

Joy is a net of love by which we can capture souls. God loves the person who gives with joy. Whoever gives with joy gives more. The best way to show, our gratitude to God and to people is to accept with joy. Joy can thrive in a heart burning with love.

We wait impatiently for the paradise where God is, but we have it in our power to be in paradise with Him, right now; being happy with Him means:

To love as He loves.
To help as He helps.

To give as He gives.
To serve as He serves.

HE MAKES THE CHOICE

| *Mother Teresa was twelve years old when she experienced the first call.**

It was in Skopje, Yugoslavia. I was only twelve years old. I was living at home with my parents. We children went to a school that was not Catholic, but we also had very good priests who helped the boys and girls to follow their vocation according to God's call. It was at that time that I knew I was called to the poor.

Between the ages of twelve and eighteen I did not want to become a nun. We were a very happy family. But at eighteen I decided to leave home for the convent, and since then, forty years ago, I have never doubted for a moment that it was the right thing for me to do. It was God's will. He made the choice.

| *It was while visiting the quarters of the poorest that she experienced a second call.*

It was a call within my vocation—a second vocation. It meant leaving the Loreto convent, where I was very happy, to go into the streets and serve the poor.

In 1946 I was going to Darjeeling to make my retreat. On the train I heard the call to give up every-

*For the beginnings of Mother Teresa's call and apostolate to the poor, see Malcolm Muggeridge's interview with her in *Something Beautiful for God,* pp. 83 ff.

thing and follow Him, to go into the slums and serve Him among the poorest of the poor.

> *Years later Bordignon asked her what had prompted her. She said simply that she didn't exactly know. And then, with a deeply human smile, as though to help him understand, she added:*

Perhaps it was a force, the Spirit of God. I knew that God wanted something . . .

> *Mother Teresa explained to Malcolm Muggeridge the steps in leaving the Loreto convent.*

First I had to apply to the archbishop of Calcutta. Then, with his approval, the Mother General of the Sisters of Loreto permitted me to write to Rome. This was the normal procedure. I was a nun; I had taken my perpetual vows, and a nun must not leave her convent. I wrote to the Holy Father, Pope Pius XII, and by return mail received an answer on April 12. He permitted me to leave and to be a non-claustral nun, that is, to live the life of a religious but under obedience to the archbishop of Calcutta. That was in 1948.

I left the convent of Loreto and went first to the Sisters in Patna to get a little medical training so that I could go into the houses of the poor. Until then, I had only done teaching. Now I had to go into the homes and see the children and the sick.

> *Mother Teresa went to look for people lying in the streets. But first she needed a place to put them.*

We needed a shelter for these most forsaken individuals. To find one, I walked, and walked, until I could walk no more. I understood then how exhausted must be the truly poor, always having to look for a little food, or some medicine, and everything. The memory of the comfort I enjoyed at the convent of Loreto then tempted me.

| *But she did not succumb.*

O God, because of my free choice and for the sake of Your love alone I want to remain here and do what Your will demands of me. No, I will not turn back. My community, they are the poor. Their security is my security; their health, my health. My home is to be with the poor, no, not the poor, but the poorest among the poorest: those who are shunned because they are infected and filthy, full of germs and crawling with vermin; those who do not go out to beg because they cannot go out naked; those who do not eat because they no longer have the strength; those who fall exhausted to the street knowing they will die, and whom the living go out of their way to avoid; those who no longer weep because they have run out of tears; the untouchables! The Lord wants me where I am. He will find a solution.

| *The first Sister to enter Mother Teresa's congregation was warned:*

You will have to renounce yourself. Your life will require constant self-denial.

| *Think it over she did, but Sister Agnes became the first Missionary of Charity. Since then, vocations*

> *have never stopped coming. Mother Teresa sees*
> *this as a sign of God's favor.*

If God gives vocations, it is a sign that He wants us to go out to the poor.

> *Mother Teresa is now sure that this work is God's*
> *work and that it will continue because:*

It is His, and not mine. That is why I have no fear. I know that if the work was mine, it would die with me. But I know that it is His work, that it will endure and do much good.

> *Does she miss the comforts of Loreto, Bordignon*
> *wanted to know.*

I was the happiest Sister in that community. And it was a great sacrifice to leave the work I was doing there, but I did not leave the religious life. The change was only in the work, since the Sisters there only taught, which is an apostolate for Christ.

But my vocation, within the vocation, was for the poorest of the poor.

> *Asked why there are so few vocations in the world,*
> *she replied:*

There is too much affluence, too much comfort, a very high standard of living, not only in families but even in the religious life.

From all parts of the world young women come to India and lead a very poor life, poorer than ours, driven by the desire to get away from their environment of riches. I believe that they really want to be a living example of the poverty of Christ. It is not enough to know the spirit of poverty; it is necessary to know poverty itself, where one literally has nothing. Today, people, even among those who come from a "good" environment, want to experience what "not having" means. The majority of vocations we have had from Europe or America asked to join our congregation, not for the work but for love of poverty.

> *One word sums up Mother Teresa: love. With the Little Flower she could say: I realized that love embodies all vocations, that love is everything, that it embraces all times and all places; in a word, that it is eternal.*

> *We do not pretend to have exhausted our subject—Mother Teresa and her work are not so easily summarized. To readers who have been touched by what they found in these pages, by Mother Teresa's appeal and example, to them we suggest that the best way to learn still more about her is by lending her not only their hearts but, in whatever way practical, a helping hand. This, among other things, is what we have tried to put across.*
> *—Editors*

> *"I am an optimist, and I am convinced that as long as there are persons like Mother Teresa, humanity can feel justified in its hope."—GIRI, President of India*

PART III

Mother Teresa Speaks to Her Religious

Delhi
20 September 1959

My Dear Sisters,

The seventh of October is a day of thanksgiving in our Society. It is the day when the Good God erected our little Society into being.

As the Society is the sole property of Our Lady, it was only right that on her great day she would grant us the grace of living and growing. It is for us to grow into a straight, beautiful, fruitful tree. Promise her that you will be a source of joy for her, just as she is the cause of our joy.

My dear children, there is so much in my heart to tell you but these two things are uppermost: charity and obedience. Be true co-workers of Christ; radiate and live His life. Be an angel of comfort to the sick, a friend to the little ones and love each other as God loves each of you with a special, most intense love. Be kind to each other. I prefer you to make mistakes in kindness than work miracles in unkindness.

Be kind in your words. See what the kindness and discretion of Our Lady brought to her. She never uttered a word of the angel's message to Joseph, and then God Himself intervened. She kept all things in her heart.

Try to excel in obedience. Now that we have three local Superiors, help them by your cheerful and prompt, blind and simple obedience. You may be more talented, more capable, better in many ways, even more holy, than your Superior. All these qualities are not required for you to obey. There is only one thing to remember: "She takes the place of God for you."

Be not blind, my children. The good God has given you His work. He wants you to do His work in His way. Failure or success mean nothing to Him, as long as you do His work according to His plan and His will. You are infallible when you obey. The devil tries his best to spoil the work of God and as he cannot do it directly to Him, he makes us do God's work in our way and this is where the devil gains and we lose.

In all our houses and in the noviciate God is blessing the generosity of the Sisters. Keep up this generosity. You have every reason to be happy. Keep smiling at Jesus in your Superiors, Sisters, and in your poor.

I must put all my energy into doing God's work well. 'I will,' said John Berchmans, Stanislaus, Margaret Mary and they did become saints.

What is a saint but a resolute soul, a soul that uses power plus action. Was not this what St. Paul meant when he said, "I can do all things in Him who strengthens me"?

With you, my Sisters, I will not be satisfied with your being just a good religious. I want you to be able to offer God a perfect sacrifice. Only holiness perfects the gift.

To resolve to be a saint costs much. Renunciation, temptation, struggles, persecutions and all kinds of sacrifices surround the resolute soul. One can love God only at one's own expense.

"I will be a saint" means: I will despoil myself of all that is not God; I will strip my heart and empty it of all artificial things; I will live in poverty and detachment. I will renounce my will, my inclinations, my whims, and fancies and make myself a willing slave to the will of God.

First Friday in November 1960

My Dearest Sisters,

On the 25th at 5:45 AM I am leaving by Pan Am and will be in America on the 26th at 6:30 AM. I go, but my heart and my mind and the whole of me is with you. It is the will of God that I should go, so let us therefore be happy. During my absence, Sister Mary Agnes, the Assistant General and the Council General will take all responsibility. God will take care of you all, if you remain one. Cling to the Society because in the center is Jesus.

I am not afraid to leave you, for I know the great gift God has given me in giving you to me. On my way back, that will be about the 15th of November, I shall go to Rome. I am going to try and see our Holy Father and beg him to grant us pontifical recognition. We are not worthy of this great gift, but if it is God's Holy will, we will get it.

During this time it would make me very happy if the seniors make sacrifices in obedience; juniors in charity; novices in poverty; and postulants in chastity.

Seniors: obedience that is prompt, simple, blind, cheerful; for Jesus was obedient unto death.

Juniors: charity in words, deeds, thoughts, desires, feelings; for Jesus went about doing good.

Novices: poverty in desires and attachments, in likes and dislikes; for Jesus, being rich, made Himself poor for us.

Postulants: chastity in thoughts and affections, in desires and attachments, in not listening to idle conversation; for Jesus is a jealous lover.

Be faithful in little things, for in them our strength lies. To the good God nothing is little because He is great and we so small. That is why He stoops down and takes the trouble to make those little things to give us a chance to prove our love for Him. Because He makes them, they are very great. He cannot make anything small; they are infinite.

To the feet of Christ's vicar on earth I will carry each of you, and I am sure with his fatherly love he will bless each one of you.

First Friday in January 1961

My Own Dearest Children,

Fidelity to the rule is the most precious and delicate flower of love we religious can give to Almighty God. The rule is the expression of the will of God—we must submit to it everywhere and always, down to the last breath.

We must be convinced that the slightest unjustified violation wounds the heart of Jesus and stains our conscience. When the rule becomes one of our greatest loves, then this love expends itself in free and joyful service.

Submission for someone who is in love is more than a duty. This is the secret of the saints.

Fidelity in the least things, not for their own sake; for this is the work of small minds, but for the sake of the great thing, which is the will of God and which I respect greatly in little things.

St. Augustine says: "Little things are indeed little, but to be faithful in little things is a great thing." Is not Our Lord equally the same in a small host as in a great one? The smallest rule contains the will of God as much as the big things of life. To be able to understand this truth I must have faith in the rule, that it is of divine origin. I must cling to the rule as a child clings to its mother. I must love the rule with my will and reason.

It does not matter that the rule often seems unnatural, hard and austere . . . . God has been so very wonderful to us and it is our duty to be very wonderful to God.

First Friday in February 1961

My Dearest Sisters,

We all want to do something beautiful for God. ... Try to imagine all kinds of sacrifices and mortifications. Take your rules and try to live them with greater love for Jesus and with Jesus.

St. Vincent compares the rules to "wings to fly to God." A dying Sister asked: "What should have I done to be a saint?" The priest answered: "Are you not familiar with this wonderful little book, your rule? If you had lived this rule you would have been a saint."

"Just think" says St. Alphonsus, "by the discharge of your duties you may become a saint."

St. Vincent says: "Keep your rules and you will become a saint, for they are holy in themselves, they also can make you holy."

St. Francis de Sales writes: "Walk on always in the punctual observance of your rules, and you will be blessed by God, for He Himself will lead you with great care." In the observance of the rule, you will find strength for the purity of conscience, fervor to fill your soul, and love that will inflame your heart.

Bauthier says: "The rule is to our will what the arteries are to our blood."

22 April 1961

My Dearest Sisters,

When you go to heaven, Our Lord is not going to ask you, "Was your Superior holy, clever, understanding, cheerful, and so forth?" but only one thing, "Did you obey me?" What a wasted life is ours if it is so full of self instead of Him, your spouse whose place she takes. If you cannot see Jesus in your Superior how will you see Jesus in the poor? How will you find Jesus in His distressing disguise? How will you love Jesus you cannot see, if you do not love your Superior whom you can see? When the devil is angry with the work of love of God and does not know how to spoil it, he will try to spoil the instruments and so indirectly spoil the work of God. Do not allow yourselves to be deceived. Obey fully, obey because you love Jesus. Obey, obey. It does not matter who they are and what they are, as long as they are He for whose sake you obey.

See how Our Lady obeyed the angel: "Be it done to me according to Thy word." Whose word? The angel's, because he took the place of God. She, the Queen of Heaven, obeys the angel. See how she obeyed St. Joseph. To her, St. Joseph was He whose place he took.

First Friday in June 1961

My Dearest Sisters,

Do not imagine that love to be true must be extraordinary. No, what we need in our love is the continuity to love the One we love. See how a lamp burns, by the continual consumption of the little drops of oil. If there are no more of these drops in the lamp, there will be no light, and the Bridegroom has a right to say: "I do not know you."

My children, what are these drops of oil in our lamps? They are the little things of everyday life: fidelity, punctuality, little words of kindness, just a little thought for others, those little acts of silence, of look and thought, of word and deed. These are the very drops of love that make our religious life burn with so much light.

Do not search for Jesus in far off lands; He is not there. He is in you. Just keep the lamp burning and you will always see Him.

First Friday in July 1961

My Dearest Sisters,

I did feel very happy to be able to give the Sacred Heart a new tabernacle in Asansol as a token of gratitude to Rev. Fr. C. Van Exem. . . . Without our suffering, our work would be just social work, very good and helpful, but it would not be the work of Jesus Christ. Jesus Christ wanted to help by sharing our life, our loneliness, our agony and death, and all that in the darkest night. . . .

All the desolation of the poor people, their material poverty, their spiritual destitution might be redeemed by our sharing it, by our being one with them, by bringing God into their lives and bringing them to God.

First Friday in August 1961

My Dearest Children,

. . . How great is our calling. How fortunate people would think themselves if they were given a chance to give personal service to the King of this world. And here we are—we can touch, serve, love Christ all the days of our lives . . .

Your work for the poor will be done better if you know the way God wants you to do it and you will know this only through obedience. Cling to your Superiors as the creeper clings. The creeper can live and grow only if it clings on something. You also will grow and live in holiness only if you cling to obedience.

First Friday in June 1962

My Dearest Children,

One day St. Margaret Mary asked Jesus: "Lord, what will Thou have me to do?"

"Give me a free hand," Jesus answered.

Let Him empty and transform you and afterwards fill the chalice of your hearts to the brim, that you in your turn, may give of your abundance. Seek Him. Knowledge will make you strong as death. Love Him trustfully without looking back, without fear. Believe that Jesus and Jesus alone is life. Serve Jesus, casting aside and forgetting all that troubles or worries you, make loved the love that is not loved.

Mother House
4 August 1962

My Dearest Children,

Let us beg Our Lady to make our hearts "meek and humble" like her Son's was. It was from her and in her that the heart of Jesus was formed. We learn humility through accepting humiliation cheerfully. We have been created for greater things; why stoop down to things that will spoil the beauty of our hearts? How

much we can learn from Our Lady! She made use of
the Almighty Power that was in her. Tell Our Lady to
tell Jesus "They have no wine," the wine of humility
and meekness, of kindness, of sweetness. . . .

First Friday in November 1962

My Dearest Children,

The first lesson of the heart of Jesus is our examina-
tion of conscience. "Know thyself." Examen is a part-
nership between us and Jesus. We should not rest in
useless looks at our own miseries, but should lift our
hearts to God and His light. . . .

. . . In our vow of obedience, is there no lessening of
our faith, seeing the human limitations of our Superior?

Our obedience, by being prompt, simple, and cheerful, is the proof of our faith. If God loves a cheerful
giver how much more would He not love an obedient
giver. . . . Obey as Christ obeyed. . . . He saw the will
of His Father—in everything and everybody—so He
could say "I do the things that are pleasing to Him."
He obeyed Caiaphas and Pilate because authority was
given from "above." He submitted to them with obedience and dignity. He did not look at the human limitations of Caiaphas and Pilate.

Mother House
19 May 1963

My Dearest Children,

The greatness of Our Lady was in her humility. No
wonder Jesus, who lived so close to her, seemed to be

so anxious that we learn from Him and her but one lesson—to be meek and humble of heart.

Humility is truth, therefore in all sincerity we must be able to look up and say: "I can do all things in Him who strengthens me." By yourself you can do nothing, have nothing but sin, weakness and misery. All the gifts of nature and grace, you have them from God. . . . Why allow temptations against your vocation?

10 November 1963

My Dearest Children,

This year we must prepare a better crib, a crib of poverty. It will be easy to fill the emptiness of the crib with charity.

We think we know ourselves enough. Our very lives are all for God, therefore why spend so much time on our spiritual life? It is not that we do not make our examen; no, we do it but do it alone. We have to do it with Christ if we want to make it real. Jesus is our co-worker.

Our souls should be like a clear glass through which God can be seen. Often this glass becomes spotted with dust and dirt. To remove this dirt and dust we make our examen, so that we become once more "clean of heart." He can, and He will help us to remove the "dirt and dust" if we allow Him to do it, with a sincere will to let Him have His way. Perhaps something has been lacking in us. Our vows, our duties, the virtues, our attitude to and our contacts with our neighbors . . . provide us with food enough for reflection. If we examine ourselves and find nothing to engage our attention, we need Jesus to help us detect our infidelities.

Our examen is after all the mirror we hold up to our nature, a poor weak human nature, no doubt, but one that needs the mirror to reflect faithfully all its deficiencies. If we undertake this work more sincerely, perhaps we shall find what we thought were stumbling blocks transformed by Him into stepping stones.

February 1964

My Dearest Children,

Our life has all the more need of humility since it is so much in the public eye. People surround us with love to guarantee the fruitfulness of our works of charity. It is beautiful to see the humility of Christ "who being in the form of God, thought it not only robbery to be equal with God, but emptied Himself, taking the form of a servant being made in the likeness of man and found in habit as a man."

... People do not want proud Sisters, for they are like a heavy instrument in the hands of God. The poor too want to be treated like children of God, not like slaves. ...

It is a great virtue to practice humility without our knowing that we are humble.

March 1964

My Dearest Children,

... There is only one true prayer, only one substantial prayer: Christ Himself. There is only one voice that rises above the face of the earth: the voice of Christ. . . .

3 June 1964

My Dearest Children,

. . . It is said that humility is truth and Jesus is the Truth, therefore the one way that will make us most Christlike is humility. Do not think that hiding your gifts of God is the sign of humility. No, do and use whatever gifts God has given you.

Mother House
15 August 1964

My Dearest Sisters,

Today will be one of the most beautiful feasts of Our Lady. She fulfills her role as cause of our joy. Do we really know why we love Our Lady so much? Because she was the spotless mirror of God's love. . . . Are we afraid of sin? . . . How terrible sin must be, if it has the power to kill God's life in us, for mortal sin kills, it causes a mortal wound in the heart of God in us. Let us die rather than ever wound God mortally.

If venial sin is deliberately allowed to become a daily bread, it causes moral anemia and the spiritual life begins to crumble and fall apart. . . .

Claude de La Colombière writes: "We see after one, two or three years, that the cowards are still cowardly, the irregular are still irregular, the angry ones have acquired no gentleness, the proud no humility, the lazy no fervor, the selfish no detachment

from selfishness; that communities that ought to be
fiery furnaces, where they would unceasingly burn
for love of God and where the soul would become so
Christlike, so near to God, remain frightfully medio-
cre."

Mother House
1 November 1964

My Dearest Children,

I come again and again to the same point: silence
and charity. Silence of the tongue will teach us so
much, to speak to Christ. Silence of the eyes will always help us to see God. Our eyes are like two win-
dows through which Christ or the world comes to our
hearts? Often we need great courage to keep them
closed. . . .

The silence of the heart, like Our Lady kept all
these things in her heart.

Mother House
15 February 1965

My Dearest Sisters,

We who are wedded to Christ cannot allow any
other love into our hearts without drawing down
God's displeasure upon ourselves. God has chosen us.
He also has the right to stop choosing us, but He will
never do it of His own accord except when we force
Him to do it.

. . . Do not play with your vocation, for when you
want to preserve it, you will not find the courage to do
so. Why do we have so many broken homes? Because

of uncontrolled affections, wanting to have all the pleasures, two loves.

. . . When we left home to enter the religious life, our parents made great sacrifices to let us go and when we are unfaithful to our vocation it grieves them deeply.

"I would be happy today if her coffin had left this house," the family of a Sister who had left told me.

Mother House
27 June 1965

My Dearest Children,

The fruit of our union with Christ is the vow of charity, just as the child is the fruit of the sacrament of matrimony. . . . Just as the lamp cannot burn without oil, so the vow of charity cannot live without the vows of poverty and obedience. . . .

San Felipe
6 August 1965

My Dearest Children, Sisters and Brothers,

From Our Lady we will ask for a delicate love for God's poor. . . . Here we have real. spiritual slums. . . .

Cocorote
5 July 1966

My Dearest Sisters,

. . . Smiling novices, I can hear the music of your laughter of joy right here in Venezuela.

Zealous young professed, the sound of your footsteps in search of souls must be like a sweet music for Jesus. Humble students, keep this Light of Christ, the lamp burning across your books, ever full of oil, so that you may become a true light of Christ in the slums.

Waltair
31 October 1966

My Dearest Children,

It is our emptiness and lowliness that God needs and not our plenitude. These are a few of the ways we can practice humility:

Speak as little as possible of oneself.
Mind one's own business.
Avoid curiosity.
Do not want to manage other people's affairs.
Accept contradiction and correction cheerfully.
Pass over the mistakes of others.
Accept blame when innocent.
Yield to the will of others.
Accept insults and injuries.
Accept being slighted, forgotten, and disliked.
Be kind and gentle even under provocation.
Do not seek to be specially loved and admired.
Never stand on one's dignity.
Yield in discussion even though one is right.
Choose always the hardest.

Mother House
13 June 1967

My Dearest Sisters,

Make it a special point to become God's sign in your community. We must radiate the joy of being poor but do not speak about it. Just be happy to be poor with Christ. . . .

Air India Across the Ocean
17 September 1967

My Dearest Children,

Once again I am crossing the ocean to prepare the way for you in search of God's poor.

Don Marmion says: "All you have to do is to leave yourself absolutely in His hands, like wax, for He cuts away mercilessly all the unnecessary parts." And when temptation to leave the order came to him he prostrated himself before the tabernacle and cried out: "Let me be cut to pieces rather than leave the monastery."

Are we strong enough to prefer being cut to pieces rather than give up Christ?

We do not change our profession as we change our clothes. Nowadays everything is getting looser and looser. People are trying to loosen the most sacred bindings. Are we to be guided by them or will we cling to the rock, Christ? . . .

Mother House
12 April 1968

My Dearest Children,

. . . Work without love is a slavery. The church
wants "renewal." Renewal does not mean the chang-
ing of habit and a few prayers. A renewal should be
faithfulness to the spirit of the Constitutions.

Mother House
18 May 1968

My Dearest Children,

We must feel the suffering of our people. To be
transfigured we have to be disfigured in our own sight.

Mother House
18 July 1968

My Dearest Children,

Offer to God every word you say, every movement
you make. We must more and more fall in love with
God. Let it not be said that one single woman in the
whole world loves her husband better than we do
Christ.

Mother House
28 January 1969

My Dearest Superiors and Sisters,

See the compassion of Christ toward Judas. The
Master who kept the "sacred silence" would not
betray him to his companions. Jesus could have

easily spoken in public and told the hidden intentions and deeds of Judas. Rather He showed mercy instead of condemning him. He called "Friend" and if Judas would have only looked into the eyes of Jesus, today Judas would have been the friend of God's mercy.

Mother House
7 May 1969

My Dearest Sisters,

These are very difficult times in the church. Do not get mixed up in gossip conversations. You hear of priests and nuns leaving and of many broken homes, but do not forget there are thousands and thousands of priests and nuns and happy families faithful unto death. This trial will purify the church of her human infirmities and she will come out of it beautiful and true.

Mother House
25 November 1969

My Dearest Children,

Next week we begin with the church the season of Advent. It is like springtime. He comes like a little child so much in need of His mother. Let us see and touch the greatness that fills the depths of their humility, Jesus' and Mary's. If we really want God to fill us we must empty ourselves through humility of all that is selfishness in us.

Mother House
19 February 1970

My Dearest Children,

The first week of Lent is nearly over. He still keeps looking for "one" to console Him. Do you try to be that "one"? Today Christ, in His vicar and the church, is being humiliated through pride in acts of disobedience and disloyalty, scourged by evil tongues.

He is thirsty for the kindness He begs from you, naked for the loyalty He hopes of you.

Today much of the suffering in the church and outside of it is caused solely by misunderstood notions of freedom and renewal. We cannot be free unless we are able to surrender our will freely to the will of God. We cannot renew unless we have the humility and the courage to acknowledge what is to be renewed in us. Therefore, be careful of people who come to you with wonderful speeches on freedom and renewal; they actually deceive and take away from you the joy and peace of Christ, the Life.

Mother House
14 March 1970

My Dearest Children,

Calcutta is really sharing in the Passion of Christ. It is sad to see so much sorrow in our beloved Calcutta. But just like Christ who after the Passion rose to live forever, so Calcutta will rise again and be the Mother of the Poor. . . . Shanti Nagar is really growing into a beautiful Town of Peace. . . .

Plane to New York
11 October 1970

My Dearest Children,

. . . Instead of spending their days in fear and trembling, our Sisters in Amman prayed the rosary continuously and the result was that on the ninth day the troops stopped near our place—peace has been proclaimed. . . .

. . . Today in the words of our Holy Father every Missionary of Charity must be able "to cleanse what is dark." . . .

Mother House
17 January 1971

My Dearest Children,

. . . The award* was most unexpected and so I had no chance to let you know in time as I knew only on the 23rd when I returned from Amman.

. . . Jesus wants to live the Truth in us and through us. . . . Speak the truth, think the truth, act the truth with God, with His church, with each other and with yourselves. Do not be surprised at each other's failure. . . . Try to see and accept that every Sister is a branch in Christ the Vine. The same life-giving sap that flows from the Vine (Jesus) through each of the branches (Sisters) is the same.

*The Pope John XXIII Peace Prize.

7 March 1971

My Dearest Children,

Sacrifice, to be real, must empty us of self. We often pray "Let me share with you Your pain" and yet when a little spittle or thorn of thoughtlessness is given to us, how we forget that this is the time to share with Him His shame and pain.

If we could but remember that it is Jesus who gives us the chance through that certain person or circumstance to do something beautiful for His Father.

Superiors: try to look and see Jesus in your Sisters. Your Sisters are His in a special way because He has chosen them and given them to you to take care of and lead them through holiness to His heart. Love them as you love Christ.

Sisters: look up and see Jesus in your Superiors. Your superior is the vine and you are a branch, and unless you and they are one and allow His Father, the Gardner, to prune you, through suffering and trials, through bearing each other's burdens, neither of you will be able to bring any fruit.

The tenth of September will be the twenty-fifth anniversary of our Society. You could not show deeper gratitude than by thinking and speaking of the goodness of each other—appreciating the good your Sisters are doing, accepting each other as you are and always meeting each other with a smile.

Mother House
29 April 1971

My Dearest Children,

The news of Bangladesh seems to become worse day by day. Hatred and selfishness are destroying a whole nation.

Today when our people are being tortured and suffer untold pain, let us reflect and avoid anything that may cause deep wounds in the hearts of the poor.

We have no right to use what belongs to the poor. We eat nothing in the houses of the rich so as to be able to tell the poor when they offer us a drink: "We do not take anything outside . . ."

They love to see the Sisters in the company of Mary, rosary in hand, always making haste to bring the good news.

10 August 1971

My Dearest Children,

. . . May our Mother be a mother to each one of us and so the cause of our joy. And may each one of us be Jesus to her and so become the cause of her joy. No one learned the lesson of humility as well as Mary did. She was the handmaiden. To be a handmaiden is to be at someone's disposal—to be used according to someone's wish—with full trust and joy. Cheerfulness and joy were Our Lady's strength. Only joy could have given her the strength to go in haste over the hills of Judea to do the work of handmaiden to her cousin. So let us go in haste over the hills of difficulties.

Franciscan Handmaids of Mary Convent
15 West 124th Street, New York
15 October 1971

My Dearest Children,

The Negro Sisters have given us a separate part of their building and this will be our convent with a lovely chapel. . . .

The news of Calcutta's cyclone is so hard to accept. Our poor people are becoming poorer day by day. Be kind to them, be a comfort to the poor and take every trouble to help them. Open your eyes to the needs of the poor.

P.S. (By Sister Andrea).—The prize our Mother received was a big heavy glass vase with a silver foot and these words engraved on it:

"The Great Seraph RAPHAEL, Mightiest of Angels, Patron of Science and Healing, whose hand stirred the waters of the Pool at Bethsaida, Protector of the Young Tobias, Helper of the Patriarch Abraham, Paragon of Knowledge and Love.

To Mother Teresa, whose struggles have shaped Something Beautiful for God.

1971 Kennedy International Award."

Mother House
3 December 1971

My Dearest Children,

Love begins at home. Do not be afraid to love until it hurts.

Love your Superiors. The Society will be what you

together with your Superior make it: a fervent or a tepid, a fruitful or a dry branch.

Mother House
26 February 1972

My Dearest Children,

We have been asked by the government of Bangladesh to take care of the girls who have been misused. I want to draw your attention to the sentence Mujibur Rahman said on behalf of these girls: "They will be treated as heroines of the country because they suffered so much to protect their purity." These girls, Hindu and Muslim, out of their natural love for purity fought to protect themselves. Many committed suicide rather than lose the beautiful virtue of womanhood.

We religious who have a chance to consecrate that beautiful gift to God in loving Him with undivided love, do we really take all the trouble to protect it and make it grow in beauty and strength?

. . . During this Lenten season we will take as a special point: Forgiveness. If we do not forgive then it is a sign that we have not been forgiven.

Sister M. Francis Xavier met with a terrible car accident but thank God, as she says: "Our Lady took care of me." She was saying the rosary and had the rosary in hand when she gained consciousness.

Mother House
19 March 1972

My Dearest Children,

Today when everything is questioned and changed, let us go back to Nazareth. How strange that Jesus should spend thirty years doing nothing, wasting His time, not giving His personality or His gifts a chance! We know that at the age of twelve He silenced the learned priests of the Temple, who knew so much and so well. Then for thirty years we hear no more of Him. No wonder the people were surprised when He came in public to preach; He was known only as a carpenter's son.

We hear so much of "personality," of "maturity," of "maternalism," and so forth, . . . and yet the Gospel is so full of words such as "little children" used by Jesus when addressing His grown-up apostles.

Mother House
28 June 1972

My Dearest Children,

Let us ask the Sacred Heart for one very special grace: love for Our Lady. Ask Him to give and deepen our love and make it more personal and intimate for her:

To love her as He loved her.
To be a cause of joy to her as He was.
To keep close to her as He kept.
To share with her everything, even the cross.

Each one of us has our cross to bear, for this is the sign that we are His. Therefore we need her to share it with us. . . .

. . . Holiness is not a luxury but a simple duty for you and me. Very great holiness becomes very simple if we belong fully to Our Lady. . . .

. . . I am sure each one of us has much to thank God:

For all the tiring journeys we have made by road, by train, by plane, by cycle in search of souls.
For all the joy we have tried to spread throughout the world.
For letting us give Our Lady full liberty to use us.

Mother House
15 August 1972

My Dearest Children,

This is my feastday greeting to each one of you: that you may know each other at the breaking of bread and love each other in the eating of this Bread of Life.

When communicating with Christ in your heart during the partaking of the Living Bread, remember what Our Lady must have felt when the Holy Spirit overpowered her and she became full with the Body of Christ. The Spirit in her was so strong that immediately she "rose in haste" to go and serve.

At the breaking of bread they recognized Him. Do I recognize the beauty of my Sisters, the spouses of Christ? Our Lady was full of God because she lived for God alone, and yet she thought of herself only as the handmaiden of the Lord. Let us do the same.

Mother House
13 December 1972

My Dearest Children,

Let us all be very much aware of the responsibility we must share together in building up our Society as a living and fruitful branch of the Body of Christ. . . .

Jesus has warned us already: "Woe to the world because of scandals. For it must needs be that scandals come; but nevertheless woe to the one by whom the scandal comes" (Matthew 18:7).

Woe to her through whom scandals are made, wrong attitudes and worldliness being very much contrary to the poverty and obedience of Christ we have chosen. It would be a shame for us to be richer than Christ, Who being rich became poor and was "subject to them."

August 1973

My Dearest Children,

I wish you the joy of Our Lady, who because she was humble of heart could hold Jesus for nine months in her bosom. What a long Holy Communion!

Rome
24 October 1973

My Dearest Children,

So many of our Sisters' parents, brothers and sisters have gone home to God during these years. I am sure they are making a new group of Co-Workers in Heaven. . . .

. . . In Ostia, there is a terrible poverty, not hunger for food but for God. People are starving for the knowledge of God.

In Yemen, our Sisters have their hands full in spite of not yet knowing the language. One of the government officials wrote: "A new era of light and love has started in Yemen."

Mother House
14 December 1973

My Dearest Children,

Our Holy Father has proclaimed the Holy Year as Year of Reconciliation. Reconciliation begins not first with others but with ourselves. It starts by having a clean heart within. A clean heart is able to see God in others. The tongue, the part of our body that comes in such close contact with the Body of Christ can become an instrument of peace and joy or of sorrow and pain. . . . Forgive and ask to be forgiven; excuse rather than accuse. . . .

25 February 1974

My Dearest Children,

Our lives should be more and more pervaded by a profound faith in Jesus, the Bread of Life, which we should partake of with and for the poor. . . .

The Sisters assure you all of their overflowing love: from Yemen, Ostia, Addis Ababa, Lima, Gaza, Coimbatore, Vijayawada, Shivpur, Tiljala, Takda, all the new homes send you their prayers. . . .

Are we truly attempting to be the poorest of the poor? In poverty which is liberty, charity increases.

Easter, 1974

My Dearest Children,

Jesus has chosen each and every one of you to be His love and His light in the world. . . .

The spirit of sacrifice will always be the salt of our Society. . . .

PART IV

Living with the Poor and Like the Poor

Mother Teresa's Commentary on the Constitution of the Missionaries of Charity (Unpublished Documents)

"I thirst," Jesus said on the Cross. He spoke of His thirst not for water but for love.

Our aim is to quench this infinite thirst of God made man.

So the Sisters, using the four vows of chastity, poverty, obedience and wholehearted free service to the poorest of the poor, ceaselessly quench that thirsting of God.

"Nothing common" wrote St. Ignatius to the scholastics, "can satisfy the obligations by which you have bound yourselves to striving after perfection. Consider your vocation, of what character it is, and you will see what might be satisfactory in others is not so in your case."

Let us remember the words of St. Theresa of Lisieux: "How shall I show my love, since love shows itself by deeds?" Well, the little child Theresa will strew flowers: "I will let no tiny sacrifice pass, no look, no word. I wish to profit by the smallest actions and to do them for love. . . . I will sing always even if my roses must be gathered from amidst thorns and the longer and sharper the thorns, the sweeter shall be my song."

"Our Lord," she said, "has need of our love; He has no need of our works."

The same God who declares that He has no need to tell us if He be hungry did not disdain to beg a little water from the Samaritan woman. He was thirsty, but when He said "Give me to drink," He, the Creator of the Universe, was asking for the love of His creatures.

To become a saint, one must suffer much. Suffering begets love . . . and life among the souls.

For us, the carriers of God's love, how full of love we must be in order to be true to our name.

Let us always remain with Mary our Mother near our crucified Jesus, with our chalice made of the four vows and filled with the wine of self-sacrifice.

All our actions, therefore, must tend to advance our own and our neighbor's perfection by nursing the sick and dying, by gathering and teaching little street children, by visiting and caring for beggars and their children, and by giving shelter to the abandoned.

To labor at the conversion and sanctification of the poor in the slums means hard ceaseless toil, without counting the results or the cost.

To convert is to bring to God. To sanctify is to fill with God. To convert and sanctify is the work of God, but God has chosen in His great mercy the Missionaries of Charity to help Him in His own work. It is a special grace granted to the Missionaries of Charity with no merit on their part to carry the light of Christ into the dark holes and slums.

Those, therefore, who join the Institute are resolved to spend themselves unremittingly in seeking out in towns and villages, even amid squalid surroundings, the poor, the abandoned, the sick, the infirm, the dying.

Zeal for souls is the effect and the proof of true love of God. We cannot but be consumed with the desire for saving souls. Zeal is the test of love and the test of zeal is devotedness to His cause, spending life and energy in the work of souls. . . .

It cannot be denied that the active life is full of dangers, because of the numerous occasions of sin to which it gives rise, but let us be sure of God's special protection in all our works assumed under obedience. To hesitate when obedience calls us to action would be to deserve the rebuke Peter merited, "O thou of little faith, why didst thou doubt . . ."

Our Lady arose and went with haste to the hill country . . . and Mary remained about three months to do the work of a servant for her old cousin. . . . We must possess before we can give. She who has the mission to distribute must first increase in the knowledge of God and fill herself with the knowledge God wishes to grant to souls through her agency.

"Before allowing his tongue to speak, the apostle

ought to raise his thirsting soul to God and then give forth what he has drunk in, and pour forth what he has been filled with," says St. Augustine.

St. Thomas tells us: "Those who are called to the works of the active life would be wrong in thinking that their duty exempts them from the contemplative life." This duty adds to it. Thus these two lives, instead of excluding each other, call for each other's help, implement and complete each other. Action to be productive has need of contemplation. The latter, when it gets to a certain degree of intensity diffuses some of its excess on the first.

. . . When there is need of speaking, we must not be afraid. He will tell us what and how to say the things He wants us to say.

Christ must be preached to pagans that they may know him, to heretics and schismatics that they may return to His fold; to bad Catholics that they may be drawn by His mercy; to the good and the pious that they may in His love be consumed and live His life.

Mary, under her divine Son, has sovereign dominion in the administration of supernatural graces and benefits of God's kingdom. She is our Mother because in her love she cooperated in our spiritual rebirth. She continues to be our Mother by nourishing the life of Christ in us.

Holiness increases in proportion to the devotion that one professes for Mary. The way back to God is through sinlessness and purity of life. Mary the Immaculate One is the way. She, "our life, our sweetness and our hope," is the way to peace. Pope Pius XII first consecrated the world to the Immaculate Heart of Mary on 31 October 1942. "There will be peace if the devotion to the Immaculate Heart of Mary is established throughout the world." This Our Lady promised to the three children of Fatima.

Charity must not remain shut up in the depth of the heart, for "no man lighteth a candle and putteth it under a bushel, but on a candlestick, that it may shine for all that are in the house."

A Missionary is a carrier of God's love, a burning light that gives light to all; the salt of the earth. It is said of St. Francis Xavier that "he stood up as a fire, and his words burnt like a torch." We have to carry Our Lord in places where He has not walked before. The Sisters must be consumed with one desire: Jesus. We must not be afraid to do the things He did—to go fearlessly through death and danger with Him and for Him.

A Missionary carries the interest of Christ continually in her heart and mind. In her heart there must be the fire of divine love and zeal for God's glory. This love makes her spend herself without ceasing. This becomes her real object in life and her joy. When Brother Lievens, S. J., was told to make his fire "a lasting one" he replied "No, I must make it a burning one." He spent himself in ten years' time. Jesus says: "Amen, unless the grain of wheat falls to the ground and dies, itself remaineth alone. But if it dies it brings forth much fruit". The Missionary must die daily if she wants to bring souls to God. The title "Missionary Religious" should humble us, for we are unworthy.

Our holy faith is nothing but a Gospel of love, re-
vealing to us God's love for men and claiming in return man's love for God.

Let us "act" Christ's love among men, remembering
the words of the Imitation, "love feels no burden, val-
ues no labors, would willingly do more than it can. It
complains not of impossibilities, because it conceives
that it may and can do all things; when weary is not
tired; when straitened is not constrained; when fright-
ened is not disturbed; but like a living flame and a
torch all on fire, it mounts upwards and securely
passes through all opposition."

Charity is patient, is kind, feels no envy, is never
perverse or proud or insolent; it has no selfish aims,
cannot be provoked, does not brood over an injury; it
takes no pleasure in wrong-doing but rejoices over the
victory of the truth; it sustains, believes, hopes, en-
dures to the last. Love has a hem to her garment that
reaches the very dust. It sweeps the stains from the
streets and lanes, and because it can, it must. The
Missionary of Charity, in order to be true to her name,
must be full of charity in her own soul and spread that
same charity to the souls of others, Christians and
pagans alike.

Total surrender consists in giving ourselves completely to God, because God has given Himself to us.
If God owes nothing to us and is ready to impart to us
no less than Himself, shall we answer with just a
fraction of ourselves? I give up my own self and in this
way induce God to live for me. Therefore to possess
God we must allow Him to possess our souls. How poor

we would be if God had not given us the power of giving ourselves to Him. How rich we are now. How easy it is to conquer God. We give ourselves to Him, then God is ours, and there can be nothing more ours than God. The money with which God repays our surrender is Himself.

To surrender means to offer Him my free will, my reason, my own life in pure faith. My soul may be in darkness. Trial is the surest way of my blind surrender.

Surrender is also true love. The more we surrender, the more we love God and souls. If we really love souls, we must be ready to take their place, to take their sins upon us and expiate them. We must be living holocausts, for the souls need us as such.

There is no limit to God's love. It is without measure and its depth cannot be sounded. "I will not leave you orphans."

Now reverse the picture. There must be no limit to the love that prompts us to give ourselves to God, to be the victims of His unwanted love. We cannot be pleased with the common. What is good for others is not sufficient for us. We have to satiate the thirst of an infinite God dying of love. We cannot be content with the common lot, but with undaunted courage and fearlessness meet all perils and dangers with equanimity of soul, ever ready to make any sacrifice, to undertake any toil and labor. A Missionary of Charity must always push forward until she comes close to the King dying of thirst.

Loving trust. One thing Jesus asks of me is that I lean upon Him; that in Him alone I put complete trust; that I surrender myself to Him unreservedly. I need to give up my own desires in the work of my perfection. Even when I feel as if I were a ship without a compass, I must give myself completely to Him. I must not attempt to control God's actions. I must not desire a clear perception of my advance along the road, nor know precisely where I am on the way of holiness. I ask Him to make a saint of me, yet I must leave to Him the choice of that saintliness itself and still more the choice of the means that lead to it.

Cheerfulness should be one of the main points of our religious life. A cheerful religious is like sunshine in a community. Cheerfulness is a sign of a generous person. It is often a cloak that hides a life of sacrifice. A person who has this gift of cheerfulness often reaches great heights of perfection. Let the sick and suffering find us real angels of comfort and consolation. Why has the work in the slums been blessed by God? Not on account of any personal qualities but on account of the joy the Sisters radiate. What we have, faith and the conviction that we are the beloved children of God, people in the world have not got, much less the people in the slums. The surest way to preach Christianity to the pagan is by our cheerfulness. What would our life be if the Sisters were unhappy? Slavery and nothing else. We would do the work but we would attract nobody. This moodiness, heaviness, sadness, is a very easy way to tepidity, the mother of all evil.

If you are cheerful, have no fear of tepidity. Joy shines in the eyes, comes out in the speech and walk.

You cannot keep it in for it bubbles out. When people
see the habitual happiness in your eyes, it will make
them realize they are the loved children of God. Every
holy soul at times has great interior trials and darkness, but if we want others to realize that Jesus is
there, we must be convinced of it ourselves. Just imagine a Sister going to the slums with a sad face and
heavy step. What would her presence bring to these
people? Only greater depression.

Joy is very infectious; therefore, be always full of
joy when you go among the poor. That cheerfulness,
according to St. Bonaventure, has been given to man
that he may rejoice in God in the hope of eternal good
and at the sight of God's benefits; that he may rejoice
in his neighbor's prosperity, take a delight in praising
God and doing good works and feel disgust for all vain
and useless things.

"It would be equally extraordinary," says St. Ignatius, "to see a religious who seeks nothing but God
sad, as to see one who seeks everything but God
happy."

Nationalism is inconsistent with our Constitution.
Hence we should never fasten an unfavorable opinion
on to people belonging to a nation other than ours. We
must not defend politicians, nor should we make war
and strife the subject of our conversation if mention-
ing them harms charity. . . . Nationalism is contrary
to "Go therefore, and teach all nations" (Matthew
28:19). "Their sound hath gone forth to all the earth,"
St. Chrysostom says of St. Paul. "The heart of Paul is
the heart of the whole world." Would that the same

could be said of us. Girls of any nationality are welcome in our society.

Poverty. One loses touch with God when one takes hold of money. God preserve us. It is better to die. What would one do with surplus money? Bank it? We must never get into the habit of being preoccupied with the future. There is no reason to do so: God is there. Once the longing for money comes, the longing also comes for what money can give: superfluous things, nice rooms, luxuries at the table, more clothes, fans, and so on. Our needs will increase, for one thing leads to another, and the result will be endless dissatisfaction.

If you ever have to get things, you must buy things of cheaper quality. We must be proud of being poor. Pay attention to the little fox that sneaks in after us. We may carry water upstairs for a bath and find three buckets already full in the bathing room. Then the temptation comes to use all the water. . . .

If you have to sleep in a corner where there is no breeze, do not gasp and pant to show how much you feel it. In these little things one can practice poverty. Poverty makes us free. That is why we can joke and smile and keep a happy heart for Jesus. . . .

Some Sisters seem to be in a continual, feverish excitement about money for their work. Never give the impression to people when you beg that you are out to gather money. Let your work speak. Let your love for the people enkindle the rich people's hearts. They will give if you don't grab. Even if you have to beg, show that your heart is detached by being at ease, both when they refuse you and when they give.

A rich man of Delhi said: "How wonderful it is to see Sisters so free from the world, in the twentieth century when one thinks everything is old-fashioned but the present day."

Keep to the simple ways of poverty, of repairing your own shoes, and so forth, in short, of loving poverty as you love your mother. Our Society will live as long as that real poverty exists. The institutes where poverty is faithfully practiced are fervent and need not fear decay. We must always try to be poorer still and discover new ways to live our vows of poverty. We must think ourselves very fortunate if we get a few chances in life to practice this wonderful poverty. . . . To rejoice that others are more fortunate than we takes much virtue. . . .

When St. Francis of Assisi heard that a new rich house had been built for the brethren, he refused to enter the city. . . . We must not spend time and energy on the house by making it look attractive and beautiful. God save us from such convents where the poor would be afraid to enter lest their misery be a cause of shame to them.

When we dress ourselves we should with devotion remember what each article of the religious habit means to us: the sari with its blue band is a sign of Mary's modesty; the girdle made of rope is the sign of Mary's angelic purity; sandals are a sign of our own free choice; and the crucifix is a sign of love.

. . . Sisters shall live by begging alms. We depend entirely on the charity of the people. The Sisters should not be ashamed to beg from door to door if necessary. Our Lord Himself has promised a reward even for a cup of water given in His name. It is for His sake that we become beggars.

In fact He often endured real want, as the stories of the multiplication of the loaves and fishes and the plucking of the ears of corn on walks through the fields teach us. The thought of these instances should be salutary reminders whenever in the mission or at home our meals are meagre. . . . Our Lord on the cross possessed nothing. . . . He was on the cross that was given by Pilate. The nails and the crown were given by the soldiers. He was naked and when He died, cross, nails, and crown were taken away from Him. He was wrapped in a shroud given by a kind heart, and buried in a tomb that was not His. Yet Jesus could have died as a king and He could have risen from the dead as king. He chose poverty because He knew in His infinite knowledge and wisdom that it is the real means of possessing God, of conquering His heart, of bringing His love down to this earth.

Wholehearted free service. "What so ever you do to the least of my brethren, you do it to me. This is my commandment that you love one another." Suppress this commandment and the whole grand work of the church of Christ falls in ruins. . . .

Charity for the poor must be a burning flame in our Society. And just as when a fire ceases to burn, it is no longer useful and gives no more heat, so the day the Society loses its charity toward the poor, it will lose its usefulness and there will be no life.

Charity for the poor is like a living flame. The drier the fuel, the brighter it burns; that is, when our hearts are separated from earthly motives and completely united to the will of God, we shall be able to give free service. . . . . The more united we are to God, the greater will be our love and readiness to serve the poor wholeheartedly. The more repugnant the work or the person, the greater also must be a Sister's faith, love, and cheerful devotion in ministering to Our Lord in this distressing disguise. . . .

When we recollect that in the morning we have held in our hands an all-holy God, we are more ready to abstain from whatever could soil their purity. Hence we should have deep reverence for our own person and reverence for others, treat all with accepted marks of courtesy, but abstain from sentimental feeling or ill-ordered affections. When we handle the sick and the needy we touch the suffering Body of Christ and this touch will make us heroic; it will make us forget the repugnance.

We need the eyes of deep faith to see Christ in the broken body and dirty clothes under which the most beautiful One among the sons of men hides. We shall need the hands of Christ to touch those bodies wounded by pain and suffering.

How pure our hands must be if we have to touch Christ's Body as the priest touches Him in the appearance of bread at the altar. With what love and devotion and faith he lifts the sacred host! These same feelings we too must have when we lift the body of the sick poor.

It is seeing that made Father Damien the apostle of

the lepers, that made St. Vincent de Paul the father
of the poor. . . . Such also was the case of St. Francis
of Assisi who, when meeting a leper completely disfigured, drew back, but then overcame himself and
kissed the terribly disfigured face. The result was that
St. Francis was filled with an untold joy, and the leper
walked away praising God for his cure. St. Peter
Claver licked the wounds of his Negro slaves. St. Margaret Mary sucked the pus from a boil. Why did they
all do these things if it was not because they wanted
to draw nearer to the heart of God. . . .

Spiritual life. "I kept the Lord ever before my eyes
because He is ever at my right hand that I may not
slip."

The true inner life makes the active life burn forth
and consume everything. It makes us find Jesus in the
dark holes of the slums, in the most pitiful miseries of
the poor, in the God-man naked on the cross, mourn-
ful, despised by all, the man of suffering, crushed like
a worm by the scourging and the crucifixion.

What does the Society expect of its members? To be
co-workers of Christ in the slums. Where will we fulfill
that aim? Not in the houses of the rich, but in the
slums. That is our kingdom. That is Christ's kingdom
and ours, the field we have to work in. If a boy leaves
his father's field and goes to work in another, he is no
longer his father's co-worker. Those who share everything are partners giving love for love, suffering for
suffering. Jesus, you hve given everything, life, blood,
all. Now it is our turn. We should put everything into
the field also.

. . . Our prayers should be burning words coming forth from the furnace of a heart filled with love.

. . . In our work we may often be caught in idle conversation or gossip. Let us be well on our guard for we may be caught while visiting families; we may talk about the private affairs of this or that one and so forget the real aim of our visit. We come to bring the peace of Christ but what if, instead, we are a cause of trouble? We must never allow people to speak against their neighbors. If we find that a family is in a bad mood and is sure to start their tale of uncharitableness, let us say a fervent prayer for them and say first a few things that may help them to think a little about God; then let us leave the place at once. We can do no good until their restless nerves are at peace. We must follow the same conduct with those who want to talk with the aim of wasting our precious time. If they are not in search of God, do not argue or answer their questions; leave them. Pray for them that they may see the light, but do not waste your time.

Hear Jesus your Co-Worker speak to you: "I want you to be my fire of love amongst the poor, the sick, the dying and the little children. The poor, I want you to bring them to me." Learn this sentence by heart and when you are wanting in generosity, repeat it. We can refuse Christ just as we refuse others.

"I will not give you my hands to work with, my eyes to see with, my feet to walk with, my mind to study with, my heart to love with. You knock at the door but I will not open. . . ." That is a broken Christ, a lame Christ, a crooked Christ deformed by you. If you give this to the people, it is all they will have. If you want them to love Him, they must know Him first. Therefore, give the whole Christ, first to the Sisters, then to the people in the slums, a Christ full of zeal, love, joy, and sunshine.

Am I a dark light? a false light? a bulb without the connection, having no current, therefore shedding no radiance? Put your heart into being a bright light.

Holy Communion. If we want to have life and have it more abundantly, we must live on the flesh of Our Lord.

This needs no explanation, for who could explain "the depth of the riches of the wisdom and knowledge of God"? "How incomprehensible are His judgments," cried St. Paul, and "how unsearchable His way, for who has known the mind of the Lord?"

. . . "O Lord God, give me grace this very day really and truly to begin, for what I have done till now is nothing. . . ." The easiest form of self-denial is control over our bodily senses . . . that we may truly say with St. Paul: "One thing I do, forgetting the things that are behind and stretching forth myself to these that are before, I press toward the mark. . . ."

The danger for us is to forget that we are sinners.

Humility. Humility is nothing but truth. "What have we got that we have not received?" asks St. Paul. If I have received everything what good have I of my own? If we are convinced of this we will never raise our heads in pride.

If you are humble, nothing will touch you, neither praise nor disgrace, because you know what you are.

. . . It is one thing for me to say I am sinner, but let someone else say that about me and then I feel it—I am up in arms.

If I am falsely accused, I may suffer, but deep down there is joy, because the correction is founded on reality, if even in the smallest way.

. . . Make it possible and even easy for your Superior to treat you and operate on you like the surgeon whose knife must cause pain in order to heal. When a sculptor carves a statue, what has he in his hand? A knife, and he cuts all the time.

Self-knowledge puts us on our knees, and it is very necessary for love. For knowledge of God gives love, and knowledge of self gives humility. St. Augustine says: "Fill yourselves first and then only will you be able to give to others." Self-knowledge is very necessary for confession. That is why the saints could say they were wicked criminals. They saw God and then saw themselves—and they saw the difference. Hence they were not surprised when anyone accused them, even falsely. . . . Each one of you has plenty of good as well as plenty of bad in her. Let none glory in her success but refer all to God.

We must never think any one of us is indispensable. God has ways and means. He may allow everything to go upside down in the hands of a very talented and capable Sister. God sees only her love. She may exhaust herself, even kill herself with work, but unless her work is interwoven with love it is useless. God does not need her work. God will not ask that Sister how many books she has read, how many miracles she has worked, but He will ask her if she has done her best, for the love of Him. . . .

If you are discouraged it is a sign of pride, because it shows you trust in your own powers. Never bother about people's opinions. Be humble and you will never be disturbed. Remember St. Aloysius, who said he would continue to play billiards even if he knew he was going to die. Do you play well? Sleep well? Eat well? These are duties. Nothing is small for God.

. . . We have grown so used to each other that some think they are free to say anything to anybody at any time. They expect the Sisters to bear with their unkindness. Why not try first to hold your tongue? You know what you can do, but you do not know how much the other can bear.

Prayer: The interest of friendship that unites us, that binds the young and old, is a chain of gold, a thousand times stronger than flesh and blood, because it permits the defects of the body and the vices of the soul to be seen, while charity covers all, hides all, to offer exclusively to admiration and love the work of the hands of God. . . . He it is who in your old age desires to decorate and adorn the fair beauty of your soul with toil and grief. . . . To all the ills that assail either heart or body hold up the shield of faith and patience. In your old age you will complete for the glory of God the tower of your soul that you began to build in the golden days of your youth. And when He comes, go forth to meet Him in the company of the wise virgins, your lamp filled with oil and a flame.

Recreation is a means to pray better. Relaxation sweeps away the cobwebs in the mind. . . .

In one of her apparitions to St. Catherine Labouré, Our Lady had rings on every finger, from some of which rays shone forth while from the other rings no rays came. Our Lady explained that the rays were blessings granted by her to those who had asked for them, while the rayless rings represented graces that had not yet been asked for and given.

. . . In our Home for the Dying we understand better the value of a soul. The very fact that God has placed a certain soul in your way is a sign that God wants you to do something for him or her. It is not chance; it has been planned by God. We are bound in conscience to help him or her. When visiting the families you will meet with very much misery. Sometimes you will find a little child holding the head of the dead mother. It is then that you must use all your energy to help that little child in his sorrow.

Once there were found two little children near the dead body of their father, who had died two days before. . . . God will use you to relieve this suffering . . .

To prove that Christ was divine. . . .

Fount Paperbacks

Fount is one of the leading paperback publishers of religious books and below are some of its recent titles.

- [ ] THE GREAT ACQUITTAL Baker, Carey, Tiller & Wright   £1.50
- [ ] DANCE IN THE DARK Sydney Carter   £1.50
- [ ] THE SACRAMENT OF THE PRESENT MOMENT
      Jean-Pierre de Caussade (trans. Kitty Muggeridge)   £1.25
- [ ] ALL THINGS IN CHRIST Robert Faricy   £2.50 (LF)
- [ ] THE INNER EYE OF LOVE William Johnston   £1.75 (LF)
- [ ] CHRISTIAN REFLECTIONS C. S. Lewis   £1.50
- [ ] PAUL: THE APOSTLE Hugh Montefiore   £1.50
- [ ] GOD'S YES TO SEXUALITY Ed. Rachel Moss   £1.75
- [ ] YOURS FAITHFULLY (Vol. 2) Gerald Priestland   £1.50
- [ ] I BELIEVE HERE AND NOW Rita Snowden   £1.25
- [ ] A GIFT FOR GOD Mother Teresa   £1.00
- [ ] FOUNT CHILDREN'S BIBLE   £3.95 (LF)

All Fount paperbacks are available at your bookshop or news-agent, or they can also be ordered by post from Fount Paperbacks, Cash Sales Department, G.P.O. Box 29, Douglas, Isle of Man, British Isles. Please send purchase price, plus 10p per book. Customers outside the U.K. send purchase price, plus 12p per book. Cheque, postal or money order. No currency.

NAME (Block letters) _____

ADDRESS _____

_____

_____